Motorhome France

A Practical Guide to Touring France by Motorhome or Campervan

Julie and Jason Buckley

An OurTour Publication

Near the top of the Col de l'Iseran mountain pass in the French Alps

Front Cover Photo
The motorhome aire at Auris en Oisans, Auvergne-Rhône-Alpes.

Back Cover Photo
Moët & Chandon Champagne Vineyards near Mutigny.

First Published: **November 2019**

Last Updated: **June 2024**

Acknowledgements

Maps © OpenStreetMap contributors. Please go to *openstreetmap.org* for full license conditions.

Road sign images sourced with thanks from *en.wikipedia.org/wiki/Road_signs_in_France*

Map of French Natural Parks: Par Sémhur (talk) - File:Parcs naturels français.svg, CC BY-SA 4.0, *https://commons.wikimedia.org/w/index.php?curid=36035657*

Table of Contents

Introduction 1
Overview Map of France 1
Use of GPS Coordinates 3
What3Words Addresses 4
Why Go to France in Your Motorhome? 4
France's Love for Motorhomes 4
Ease of Access from the UK 6
The French Climate 7
French Culture 7
Vineyards 8
French Landscapes 10
France and the Romans 12
France and the World Wars 13
The Tour de France 15
Cycling and Hiking 16
You Can Take Your Dog or Cat 17
Where to Go in France and When 18
When to Go 18
The Summer Holidays 18
Winter Touring 19
The 'Shoulder' Seasons 19
Festivals and Public Holidays 20
Major Events 22
Where to Go 22
France's Regions and Departments 23
Hautes-de-France 24
Normandy 28
Brittany 33
Paris, Île de France 38
Grand Est 41
Centre-Val de Loire 43
Nouvelle-Aquitaine - The Dordogne 46
Nouvelle-Aquitaine - Atlantic Coast 49
Auvergne-Rhône-Alpes - The Alps 53

Auvergne-Rhône-Alpes - The Vercors Massif 59
Provence-Alpes-Côte-d'Azur 63
Occitanie 68
The Massif Central 72
France's Most Beautiful Villages 74
All Our Overnight Locations Mapped Out 75
Route Planning 76
Types of Road in France 76
Motorhome Speed Limits 78
To Toll or Not to Toll? 80
Finding Fast, Toll-Free Routes 82
Low-Emission Zones (The CRIT'Air Scheme) 83
Onward Touring 84
Rough Idea for Costs 86
Preparation for Your Trip to France 87
Preparation for You and Your Passengers 87
The Schengen Area and 90-in-180 Days Rule 89
Obtaining ETIAS Authorisation 89
Preparation for Your Motorhome 90
Preparation for Your Pets 93
The Animal Health Certificate (AHC) 94
Sourcing Pet Food in France 95
Booking a Pet Crossing to France 95
Crossing to France with Your Pet 96
Returning from France with Your Pet 96
Booking Your Crossing 98
Choosing Between the Tunnel and a Ferry 98
Booking a Ferry 98
Booking the Channel Tunnel (Eurotunnel Le Shuttle) 99
Towing a Trailer 100
Other Things to Consider Packing 101
Renting a Motorhome in France 102
Day-to-Day Motorhome Life in France 104
Travelling to and Using the Ferry and Tunnel 104
Check the Foreign Office and Traffic England Websites 104
EU Duty Free Allowances 104
EU Import Restrictions on Meat, Dairy and Plants 105

The Dartford Crossing 105
Overnight Stays Before Leaving the UK 105
Getting On and Off the Ferry 106
Using the Channel Tunnel (Eurotunnel LeShuttle) 109
Driving in France 111
Driving on the Right 111
Traffic Lights in France 112
Roundabouts 112
Using French Toll Roads 112
Giving Way to the Right 116
Bad Weather 117
Crawler Lanes 117
Mountain Driving 118
Finding Great Places to Stay 122
To Book or Not to Book? 122
French Campsites 123
The Aires Network 126
Camping-Car Parks (PASS'ETAPES Card) 129
Free (Wild) Camping 131
Pay-For Wild Camping: Evazion 132
The France Passion Scheme 132
House Camping 133
Free Guidebooks for Places to Stay 133
Stopovers Near the North France Ports 134
Fresh Water & Waste (Bornes and Service Points) 137
Obtaining and Using Euros 139
Coping with the Language 140
Finding Fuel in France 141
Buying Diesel and Petrol 141
Eating Well in France 145
Supermarkets 145
High Street Shopping 145
Markets and Street Food 146
Eating Out 147
Staying in Touch in France 147
Using the Internet 147

Making Phone Calls 149
Watching TV 150
Sending and Receiving Post 150
Doing Your Laundry 151
Campsite Laundries 151
Self-Service Laundrettes 151
Supermarkets 152
Tips for Handing Extreme Weather 153
Hot Weather Tips 153
Cold Weather and Ski Resort Tips 154
Windy Weather Tips 156
Staying Safe and Dealing with Problems 157
Driving Safety 157
Parking Safety 158
Personal Safety 158
Contacting the Police in a Non-Emergency 159
Finding Medical Help if You Need It 159
Making Minor Repairs Abroad 160
Handling Breakdowns 161
Handling a Road Traffic Accident 163
UK Duty Free Allowances 165
Getting the Ferry or Tunnel Home 166
Escorted Tours Abroad 167
About the Authors 167
Other Books by the Authors 168
Things Change and We Make Mistakes... 169
Reference Information 170
Useful French Words 170
Packing Checklist 171
Useful Sources of Information 183

Foreword

Hi, we're the authors, Jason and Julie Buckley, and we've been fortunate to travel across France in our campervan and motorhomes many times over the years, sharing over a decade's tours via our motorhome travel blog *ourtour.co.uk*.

We started by nipping out from the UK in our panel van for a week in Brittany with friends, building up to spending several months in France, often part of year-long tours of Europe. Having seen much of what our incredibly varied continent has to offer the motorhome traveller, France remains steadfast among our favourite countries. It's a close competition, with Greece and Norway being up there too, but France is right on the UK's doorstep, and it has it all folks.

Official motorhome parking outside the mayor's office isn't unusual in France

France is easy to get to from England, with a wide choice of ferry routes and Eurotunnel LeShuttel (the Channel Tunnel) to choose from. It's also an incredibly motorhome-friendly country with this mode of travel, and even full-time motorhome living, deeply embedded in French culture.

Landscape-wise, France has a stunning variety of vistas to immerse yourself in, from windswept beaches and rocky coves to the majesty of the snow-capped Alps to the vibrant green sweeping vineyards which flow across hillsides throughout the country.

Alongside Brittany and the Alps, Provence is a favourite region for us personally, with its impressively deep gorges, sun-baked pine forests and photogenic lavender fields.

France is an easy country to travel by motorhome. The road network is in excellent condition and, outside the cities, is eerily devoid of traffic. There are overnight parking places practically everywhere, very often within an easy walk of the nearest town or attraction. The country boasts an enormous number of campsites and aires, the latter being official non-campsite locations designed especially for motorhomes to use. A couple of thousand French businesses even welcome motorhomes to stay on their premises for free, in return for the opportunity to sell you some of their high-quality produce.

There are so many wonderful places to stay in France we've hardly ever needed to book into overnight stays or plan ahead. Instead, we've used the night before to decide where to sleep, driven the following day and, on the rare occasion we found our destination full, just found another campsite or aire nearby. The sensation of freedom we've felt as a result is hard to overstate.

Locronan, Brittany. This village has its own motorhome aire.

On our tours around the country, we come across lots of British motorhome travellers, but not as many as we might imagine such an enticing destination should attract. OK, let's crack on!

Jason and Julie Buckley

Introduction

Welcome to Motorhome France!

If you've never been abroad before in your motorhome or campervan, you've a wonderful adventure ahead of you. If you're feeling nervous about crossing *La Manche* (*The Sleeve*, French for the English Channel), we know exactly how you feel. We've done it quite a few times over the years, but still get a little edgy at the thought of boarding the ferry, remembering to drive on the right and needing to speak a few words of long-forgotten French!

Don't worry. Through this book we'll fire your imagination and build your confidence, providing all the information you need to enjoy planning your journey, and travelling around this scenic, welcoming and culturally rich country.

Overview Map of France

France is over twice the area of the UK, stretching around 600 miles from the north to the south, and the same east-west. Its landscapes range from the rugged rocky Brittany Pink Granite Coast to the sun-soaked beaches of the Côte d'Azur (the French Riviera), from the expansive wetlands of the Camargue to the high snow-capped peaks of the Alps.

In a word, France is big, but it's all easily accessible by motorhome and campervan. The shortest ferry route from Dover to Calais takes around 90 minutes, with the Channel Tunnel crossing even quicker at only 35 minutes. Ferries from Ireland take around 20 hours (from Dublin), 14 hours (from Cork) or 18 hours (from Rosslare).

Using the motorway network, driving from Calais to Chambéry in the Alps takes around 9 hours and Saint-Tropez on the Côte d'Azur is 12 to 13 hours. If you don't have time for these long drives, there are plenty of great places to visit within easy striking distance of the ferry ports in the north. Paris and Euro Disney are around a 3.5-hour drive from Calais.

The cliffs and beaches of the Opal Coast, Normandy and Brittany are all immediately accessible from the French ports. Reims, set among the Champagne vineyards, is 3 hours from Calais. The Loire châteaux are about 4 hours south of Le Havre.

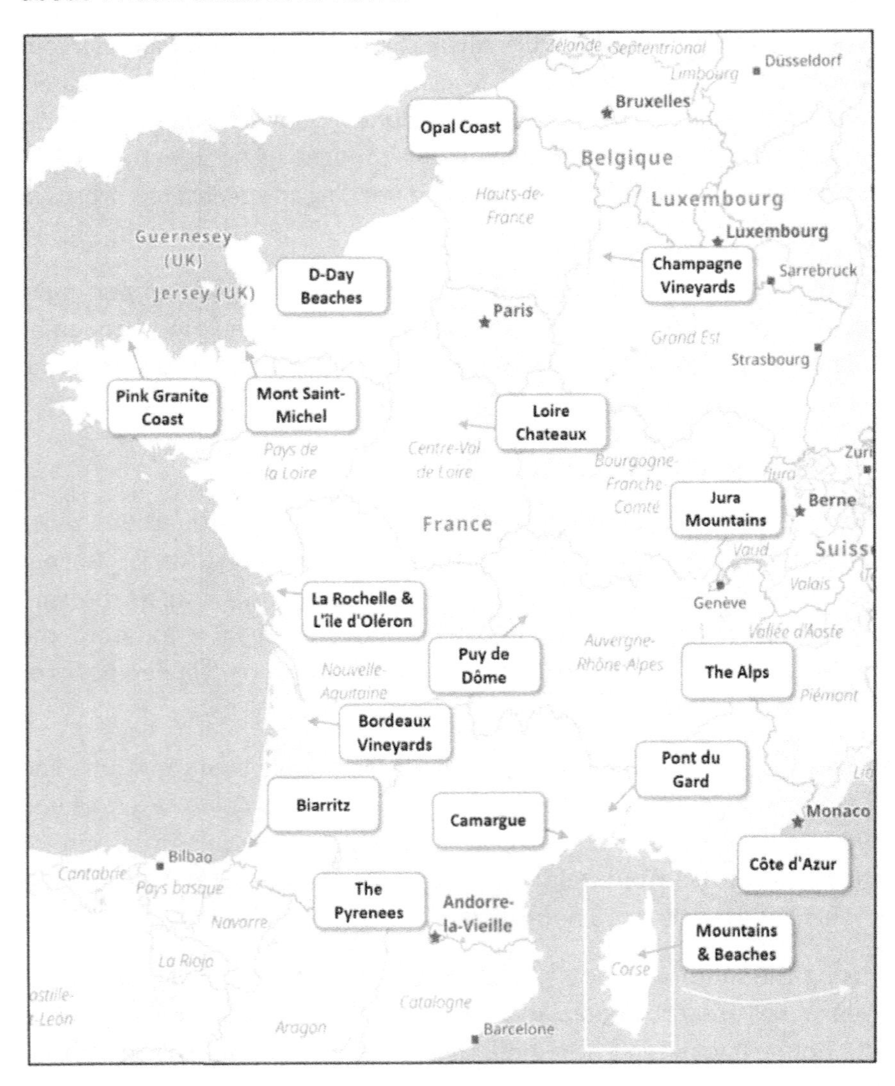

Use of GPS Coordinates

This book presents Global Positioning System (GPS) coordinates in decimal degrees ('DD' format), like this: "GPS: N48.686843, W1.36166". In some places outside this book, you might see coordinates written like this: 48.686843, -1.36166. The first number is the latitude, which is positive as all of France is in the northern hemisphere, and the second is the longitude, which might be either positive (for most of France, which sits east of the Prime Meridian at Greenwich) or negative (for those parts of France which sit to the west of the meridian).

You can either type these coordinates into your satnav or you can often just type them into an internet browser's search bar and a map will pop up showing the location. Alternatively, websites like *www.gps-coordinates.net* let you easily:

- Convert the GPS coordinates to different formats.
- View the location of the coordinates on a map.
- Virtually look around the location using Google Streetview or similar.

Viewing the location of GPS coordinates using *www.google.com*

What3Words Addresses

As well as GPS coordinates, you may also come across references to a location in this format: ///bonnet.calculating.magnum. We haven't used this format in this book, but you may see this type of address on forums, apps and so on.

These are what3words addresses. Every three-square metres across the Earth's surface is represented with a unique group of three words. You can type these into the *what3words.com* website, or the free what3words app on a smartphone, and it'll show you a map with the location it refers to. Working in reverse, you can check the app on your phone to see the three words for your current location and give them to someone else so they can see exactly where you are.

Why Go to France in Your Motorhome?

France is the most visited country in the world, welcoming around 80 million tourists each year. As well as being practically on the UK's doorstep, France is also, arguably, the most motorhome-friendly country in Europe. If you've never taken your motorhome or campervan abroad before, then you're in for a treat. The sensation of adventure in a first self-driven trip to France is unforgettable.

France's Love for Motorhomes

France has roughly the same population as the UK, but the French buy around twice as many new motorhomes each year, known locally as *camping-cars*. There are around half a million motorhomes in France, a number only exceeded by Germany (almost two million). Motorhomes are an incredibly popular means of travel and tourism in France, as well as being a full-time lifestyle for many.

The *www.lemondeducampingcar.fr* website (which translates to the World of Motorhomes) is a great resource for learning about French motorhome culture. It's in French, but you can translate it into English using Google Translate (*translate.google.co.uk*).

Sleeping among lavender at Ferme de la Condamine, Provence

There are over 10,000 campsites and 4,000 motorhome aires in France, a huge range of safe and comfortable overnight locations to suit every taste, budget and need. France's many attractions are often conveniently accessible from these, offering a stress-free method of exploring this magnificent country's culture and history.

Waiting for the Tour de France, Col de Grand Colombier

If you're looking for something more remote, there are opportunities to free camp off the beaten path. If you keep everything inside your vehicle and aren't ignoring any 'no motorhomes' or 'no overnight stays' signs, the French are pretty laid-back, and you'll be left alone to enjoy life.

A leafy French motorhome aire in Loches, Indre-et-Loire

Ease of Access from the UK

Once you've travelled to the south of England, you can be in France within a couple of hours by using the shorter ferry routes from Dover to Calais or Dunkirk, or by taking the Eurotunnel from Folkestone to Calais. Alternatively, if your departure or destination ports lie further to the west, longer ferries carry you across the Channel depositing you along the Normandy and Brittany coastlines. The ferry from Plymouth to Roscoff, for example, takes 5½ hours for day crossings or 11 hours overnight.

Once you're in France, the motorway (*autoroute*) network will take you smoothly close to wherever you want to be. Outside Brittany you'll generally need to pay tolls for these faster roads. However, there is always an alternative route available if you're not in a hurry or want to get a closer look at the country you're travelling through.

The French Climate

France's climate varies between regions, from the relatively cool and wet Brittany, to the dry summer heat of Provence and the French Riviera, to the winter snow and ice of the mountainous Alps, Central Massif and Pyrenees. As a rule, in summer expect potentially very warm weather, especially in the far south. In winter the weather isn't too different to the UK unless again you're in the far south, or up in the mountains.

Along the French Riviera on the Mediterranean coast temperatures stay mild even in deep winter, but don't expect warm evenings with temperatures dropping as low as 3°C.

A pleasant spring day at Le Tranger, Centre-Val de Loire

France also has seasonal winds which are famous (infamous) enough to have their own semi-mystical names, like *Le Mistral* and *La Bise*. If you come across one of these blowing in force, you'll know about it (the Mistral once snapped our habitation door off).

French Culture

Life in France is an easy-going affair, especially outside the big cities. Very often we'll arrive in a town to find it's 'locked o-clock', which means the shops have closed for lunch and everyone's gone to the local restaurant for the *menu du jour* or *formule du midi* (typically three-course meals with limited choices but low cost).

Compared with the UK where supermarkets are open all hours, you might be a little taken aback to find their French equivalents closed on a Sunday. On the flip side, you might also be surprised to find that even the smallest of villages has at least one *boulangerie* (bakers) sometimes sprouting a lengthy queue, and perhaps a *boucherie* too (butchers). Not all day-to-day shopping has drifted off to the out-of-town giants in France.

Buying some local cheese in Mesnières-en-Bray, Normandy

Coming from the UK the first change you might notice is just how quiet the roads are. Once you're away from the main ports, traffic seems to evaporate into thin air. More than once we've thought the road must have been closed behind us and on the opposite carriageway, as that was the only explanation for there not being a single vehicle in sight!

Vineyards

If you've ever wondered where all those French wines in the supermarket come from, why not go and have a look? France produces over eight billion bottles of wine a year from around 800,000 hectares, only Spain and China have more wine-growing area. With the France Passion scheme, described later in this book, you can get up close to the grapes directly on the vineyard, sleeping by the vines, chatting with the growers and, of course, tasting their wines!

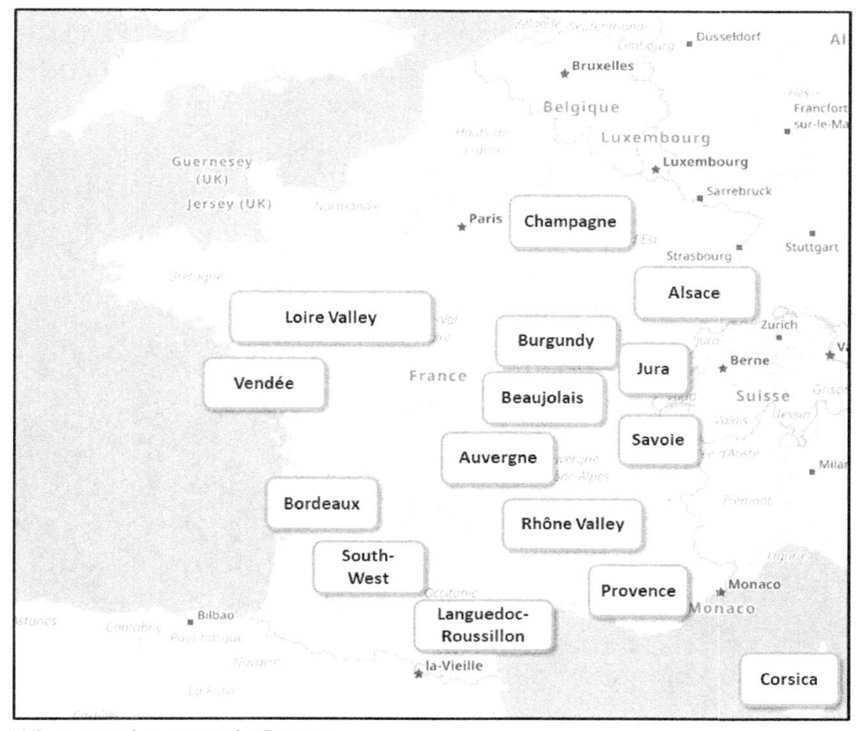

Wine growing areas in France

Champagne Vineyards, Mutigny, Marne

French Landscapes

France is awash with beautiful landscapes. Seascapes vary dramatically from the rugged coastline of Brittany to the historic D-Day beaches of Normandy, the surf-washed sands of the Atlantic coast and the chic resorts of the Côte d'Azur.

The Falaise D'Aval sea arch, Étretat, North of Le Havre

Europe's highest sand dune, the Dune du Pilat, rises from the pine forests west of Bordeaux, offering a panoramic view of the islands below. Lavender grows in rows like piped-on purple icing across the fields of Provence. The Alps rise high and majestic, echoing with marmot calls in summer and providing myriad opportunities for winter sports.

Ancient, rounded volcanoes rise in a chain like the spine of a giant in the Auvergne, where the sky is flecked with the vibrant coloured wings of paragliders. Great majestic rivers flow across France, many evocative of history like the Loire, Dordogne, Seine and Rhône. On the south coast, the Camargue wetlands offer a home to over 400 species of birds.

A view of the Mont Blanc Massif from Plaine Joux, Haute-Savoie, Alps

The Loire near Blois

France has ten national parks (seven of which are in Metropolitan France, the others are in overseas departments), and 53 regional natural parks, spread across the country. Browsing the internet for photos of these parks is a great source of inspiration, igniting a desire to travel to them, to witness these beautiful places for yourself.

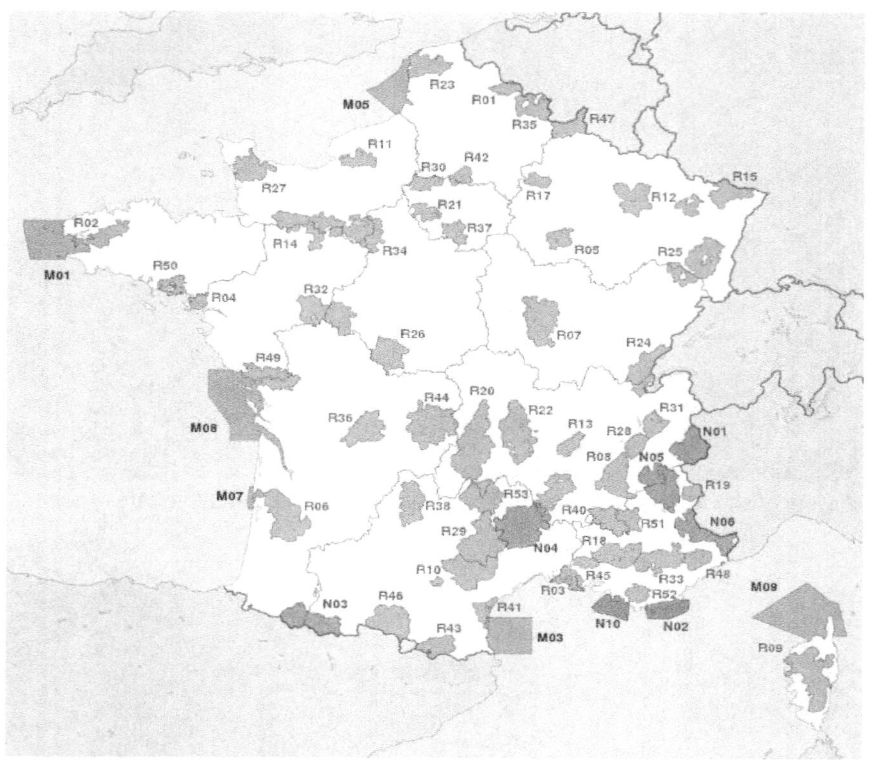

French National, Regional Nature and Marine Parks (source: Wikipedia)

France and the Romans

France was occupied by the Romans for nearly 500 years, from Julius Caesar's invasion in 58 BC up until the 5th Century AD. They left impressive and fascinating evidence of their presence, mainly in the south-east of the country.

The country's most impressive Roman remains are in and around the city of Nîmes, with its magnificent amphitheatre. We visited this city before we had our motorhome, but there's the *La Bastide* campsite four miles from the centre, plus several other overnight parking locations a bus ride from the centre of the city. Outside Nîmes, we have stayed in our motorhome in an aire within walking distance of the impressive Pond du Gard aqueduct.

The Roman amphitheatre in Nîmes

After Nîmes the town of Arles, twenty miles away, is reputed to have France's next-best Roman remains, including its own amphitheatre and theatre. Arles has an aire and campsite within walking distance of the town.

We've also visited Glanum in our motorhome, again in southern France, staying during the day in the car park for the ruins while we enjoyed walking the ancient town, set at the base of a gorge with expansive views (*www.site-glanum.fr*).

France and the World Wars

France's position in Europe made it a central battleground during the Great War and World War II. Evidence of these conflicts is marked across every inch of the country. Monuments stand in each village and town. Plaques indicate where locals or resistance fighters were killed or deported. Dramatic and thought-provoking museums, cemeteries and preserved defences provide a sombre reminder of violent times.

During our travels across France we've visited French, Commonwealth, American, German and Chinese cemeteries, the Normandy D-Day landing beaches and the WW1 battlefields around Verdun, the Chemin des Dames and the Somme. We stared in amazement at the bombproof bulk of the submarine pens at Lorient and walked the incredible underground bunker network on the Maginot Line, which the Germans bypassed in WWII by invading Belgium.

Commonwealth War Graves

Perhaps the most poignant reminder of the all-encompassing nature of war is the village of Oradour-sur-Glane, preserved as it was when 642 men, women and children were murdered by the SS in June 1944. There's an aire a short distance from the remains of the town centre.

Oradour-sur-Glane, WW2 Martyr Village, Haute-Vienne

France is proud of its resistance fighters, the *maquisards*, those who opted to struggle against German occupation and often paid a heavy price for doing so. Look out for the double-barred Cross of Lorraine, adopted as a symbol by the resistance which now stands tall at memorials.

The Mémorial de la Résistance at Chasseneuil-sur-Bonnieure in Charente

The Tour de France

Each summer the famous Tour de France cycling race flies around the country whipping up a whirlwind of excitement. Towns and villages along the route go ga-ga over the incoming race, with painted bikes tied to posts everywhere. Motorhomes line the route of the race, and in some more popular places every available inch is packed with them. These mini communities sometimes wait over a week in the best places for the world-class riders to appear.

Tour de France, Greg Van Avermaet in the Yellow Jersey

On the day of the race the road is closed a few hours before the riders arrive. The *caravane* vehicles flow through next, booming music, selling branded kit and flinging bits and bobs of free stuff out at the growing crowds. Finally, the TV helicopters buzz into view, building the spectators into a full-on frenzy of screaming and clapping as the riders finally zip past, the peloton passing in seconds on the faster flat sections (one reason many choose to spectate at mountain stages). Once the mile long tail of support cars passes, that's it all over, time to pack up and head to find a spot on the next section of the race!

Cycling and Hiking

France has a culture of supporting cycling. Riders are given patience and room on the roads, and there are thousands of miles of dedicated cycle paths to enjoy. Routes vary from gentle meanders along rivers and canals and down repurposed railway lines (green ways or *voies vertes*) to challenging mountain ascents or even downhill mountain biking parks. There are maps, cycle repair locations, route descriptions and more at *en.francevelotourisme.com*. Lonely Planet offer their *Cycling France* guide or for a paper map search for *France IGN Greenways and Cycle Routes Map 924.*

France's outstanding natural landscapes provide endless opportunities for walking, hiking and running. The AllTrails app maps out thousands of routes for all abilities, ranging from a 5km *balade* (stroll) to the Cap d'Antibes on the sun-splashed Côte d'Azur to the serious multi-day 164km Tour du Mont Blanc mountain hike (*randonnée*). The *www.gr-infos.com* site maps more long-distance (*GR* or *Grande Randonnée*) trails across France. You can hike small parts of these of course; we've enjoyed several easy out-and-back sections of the GR34 Custom Officer's path (*Sentier des Douaniers*), around the Breton coastline.

An Australian couple offer English-language inspiration, insight and advice for walking in France at *walkinginfrance.info*. If you prefer a book, Lonely Planet's *Best Day Walks France* describes and maps out 60 walks across the country with varied difficulties.

You Can Take Your Dog or Cat

Once your dog or cat has an Animal Health Certificate (AHC), or a Pet Passport if you're based in Northern Ireland, you're able to easily take them to France (and beyond) and return to the UK without any need for quarantine. The French love their pets, their supermarkets are stacked with supplies, you can often take dogs on public transport and the vets usually speak English.

You can even stay with your pets as you cross the Channel. On the Eurotunnel a train carries your motorhome under the sea with you and your pets inside (*www.eurotunnel.com*). P&O ferries between Dover and Calais have a Pet Lounge, where you can sit with your pet rather than them having to stay in your motorhome on the car deck (*www.poferries.com*). Some Brittany Ferries ships have pet-friendly cabins where you can stay on-board with your pet, currently on sails between Plymouth to Roscoff, Cork to Roscoff and Portsmouth to Caen (*www.brittany-ferries.co.uk*).

Once in France, our French neighbours will even (sometimes) welcome well-behaved dogs into restaurants and cafés. We can recall a surprising meal out with a cat casting the occasional glance at us from the next table! We travelled to France (and over 30 other countries) with our Cavalier King Charles Spaniel, imaginatively named Charlie, many times over the years.

With Charlie on the Dune du Pilat, the tallest sand dune in Europe

Where to Go in France and When

Once you've made some basic preparations for yourself, other members of your party, your motorhome and any pets you plan to take with you, the beauty of visiting France by motorhome is the lack of need to plan. Unless you have specific aims for what you want to see and do or have a specific campsite you really want to stay in, you can easily roam the country without booking a single night.

That said, the process of planning a trip can be a fun adventure in itself as the anticipation builds ahead of travel. Whether you like to plan your itinerary in detail, or wing it as you go, France will oblige. This section provides some pointers for the preparation stage of your trip.

When to Go

France is an all-season destination, but you will notice big variations in how 'alive' parts of the country feel and how busy campsites and aires are depending on when you visit.

The Summer Holidays

Reputedly every single last person abandons France's cities during the summer school holidays and takes to the coast or countryside, jamming campsites and beaches in July and August. How much truth there is in this, we're not quite sure, but it is very clear that campsites and motorhome parking areas come under much more pressure in the summer. If you do have a specific site or set of sites you want to use during the high season, it would make sense to book into them early to ensure you have a pitch.

That said, there are so many campsites and aires, as long as we're not dead set on staying in a particular spot we've always found somewhere to stay without too much trouble. When it's busy we try to arrive at our preferred aire or campsite between 10am and 2pm, for the best chance of getting a pitch. Summer peak time in France is from around Bastille Day (14th July) to the start of September.

Winter Touring

Large numbers of skiers and snowboarders head for the Alps and Pyrenees in their motorhomes (and caravans) each winter. With some preparation there's no reason you can't join them and you'll have a choice between aires located within the ski resorts or motorhome campsites with bus connections to the ski lifts.

Motorhome aires and campsites in the ski resorts get very busy during the French school holidays. France is split into three zones for the purpose of school holidays. Summer holidays are all the same, but each zone has different dates for spring and winter holidays. Check sites like *about-france.com* for the exact dates.

Outside the ski resorts expect the towns, beaches and countryside to be relatively quiet in winter. Many campsites will close, but the aires network will be quiet with plenty of space available. However, accessing fresh water is more of a challenge in winter, as the supply at service points is sometimes turned off to avoid freezing and splitting pipes.

The 'Shoulder' Seasons

Spring and the autumn are favourite travel seasons for many, as the towns and cities are still relatively lively while the weather hasn't yet turned to its coldest and greyest. Campsites and aires will be actively used but even the most popular ones will tend to have space available. Hiking will generally be pleasant, without the beating sun of summer.

Just be aware that as it gets closer to winter many small rural towns and villages in France will, pretty much, shut up shop. You can arrive to find no-one around, with hand-written signs in the shop and restaurant windows saying they're closed and will be back in the Spring.

Festivals and Public Holidays

There are lots of great *fêtes* (festivals) across France, some of which we've been lucky enough to happen across, others we've yet to experience:

- **February:** The Menton Lemon Festival takes place on the French Riviera near the Italian border. This established tradition uses over 100 tonnes of citrus fruit to decorate floats and other structures. We've not yet witnessed this spectacle but will aim for it when we're in the far south in winter.
- Between **March** and **October**, religious *pardons* take place across Brittany. They're sombre, traditional affairs, but colourful with formal masses and processions.
- **First Weekend of June:** the town of Annonay in the Ardèche department provides a heart-lifting sight as a plethora of hot air balloons (*montgolfières* in French, after the brothers who first flew a hot air balloon in Annonay) rise into the early morning sky. The town's Intermarché supermarket opposite the event allowed motorhomes to stay overnight, so we had a short walk to see the take-off.
- **21 June:** in towns and cities across France we've found the streets laden with open-air stages as musicians take part in the country-wide *La Fête de la Musique.*
- **14 July:** Most of France gets the day off to celebrate *La Fête Nationale* (Bastille Day), marking a turning point in the 18th century French Revolution. Even the smallest of villages seems to put on a firework display, sometimes accompanied with longer celebrations throughout the day, a bonfire, with bands, singing and processions.
- **December:** The *Habits de Lumière* festival takes place along the Avenue de Champagne in Épernay, under which lie around 200 million bottles of the sparkling wine. The festival was an exciting affair, with an engaging sound and light show played out on the

façade of the town hall, champagne-fuelled parties and the sight of a giant mechanised dragon stalking the avenue, its mouth full of excited children. Unforgettable. Many other cities also have *Lumière* festivals. We just missed the one in Chartres in September but hope to see it another year along with the *Fête des Lumières* in Lyon in early December.

The Annonay Hot Air Balloon Festival (*L'Art de l'Envol*)

Generally, we seem to miss the festivals by a few days or weeks. Perhaps we should be planning after all? Unless you have a specific festival you intend to visit, we'd suggest searching for 'fête' and the names of the towns and cities along your planned route, to see if anything's happening nearby. Alternatively, keep an eye out for signs as you travel, they tend to be well advertised in the host town and surrounding area.

Public holidays in France are called *jours fériés* and in most of France there are 11 of them. If they fall during the working week, then expect shops and businesses to be closed and attractions to be much busier than usual. If a bank holiday falls on a Thursday, traditionally many people take Friday off as a 'bridge day', making a four-day weekend.

Major Events

Depending on your level of interest and energy, a major event in France may be something you want to make a bee-line for, or purposefully avoid! Wherever it is, demand for overnight parking places will be at a premium and it makes sense to plan more carefully than usual. This applies especially if you want to be parked in the most popular places, where you may need to be in a place for a few days to guarantee a good spot. Here are some of France's big events with the rough time of year they take place:

- February: Nice Carnival
- February or March: Mardi Gras (carnivals are held across France)
- May: Monaco Grand Prix
- May: Cannes Film Festival
- June: 24 Hours of Le Mans (Sports Car Race)
- July: Tour de France (Cycling Race)

The France Voyage website (*www.france-voyage.com/events*) has a good list of events taking place in France, categorised by type (music, fairs and shows, gastronomy, events for children, free events and so on).

Where to Go

With a motorhome and a map, you can head to any part of France you like, making up the route as you go, going whatever twists or turns of fate lead you. On our first week and two-week long forays into France in our Talbot Autosleeper campervan we toured Brittany, managed to get as far as the Atlantic island Île de Ré, and drove up into the Vosges Mountains near the Swiss border.

The following section looks at some of the areas we've since visited and aims to give a motorhome-travel-perspective on them. Although we've spent years touring France, crossing the country north-south and east-west, we've barely scratched the surface. We'd suggest grabbing a copy of Lonely Planet France or the Rough Guide to France to get a fuller picture on where else you could visit. Bear in mind these guidebooks, by necessity of print space, limit themselves to the larger towns and attractions. France has a million smaller sights which aren't in these books but are still fascinating and often have a free motorhome aire nearby.

Each of the overnight parking locations we mention can be found in the park4night smartphone app and *park4night.com* website. If you search for the name of the relevant town and locate it on the map, you'll see the various aires, campsites and parking areas. We tend to choose ones with the highest user review rating. Many of the locations are also listed in the other books, websites and apps mentioned in the *Finding Great Places to Stay* section on page 122.

France's Regions and Departments

Metropolitan France (which includes Corsica, but not France's other overseas territories) is made up of 13 regions, which themselves contain a total of 95 departments. The departments are individually numbered with a two-digit code, which is shown on car number plates, for example, to show where a vehicle was first registered.

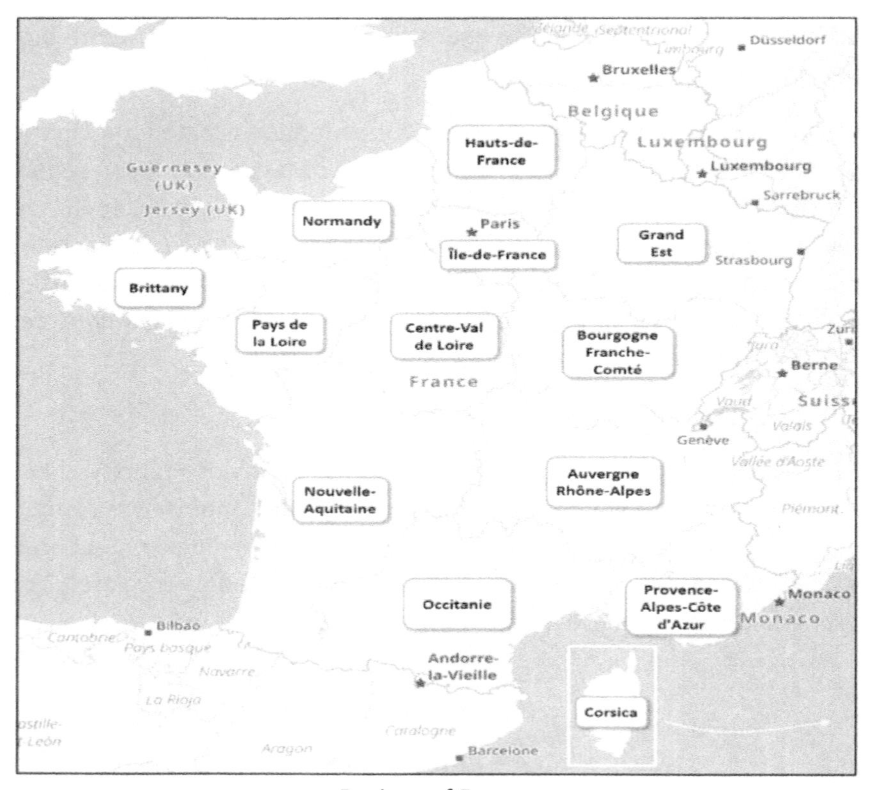

Regions of France

From a motorhome touring perspective, you'll come across the regions while planning as guidebooks all reference them. Other than that, and the fact you'll spot the signs alongside the road as you drive between them, they won't have much impact on your day-to-day travels.

Hautes-de-France

For many motorhome travellers to France the area around Calais is their first taste of the country. We've been guilty in the past of dismissing this area, flowing past it on the A16 and off into what we thought of as 'the real France'. We've since come to love the area around the Opal Coast, which is as French as anywhere in France of course, covering the area from Bray Dunes near Belgium to Berck-sur-Mer.

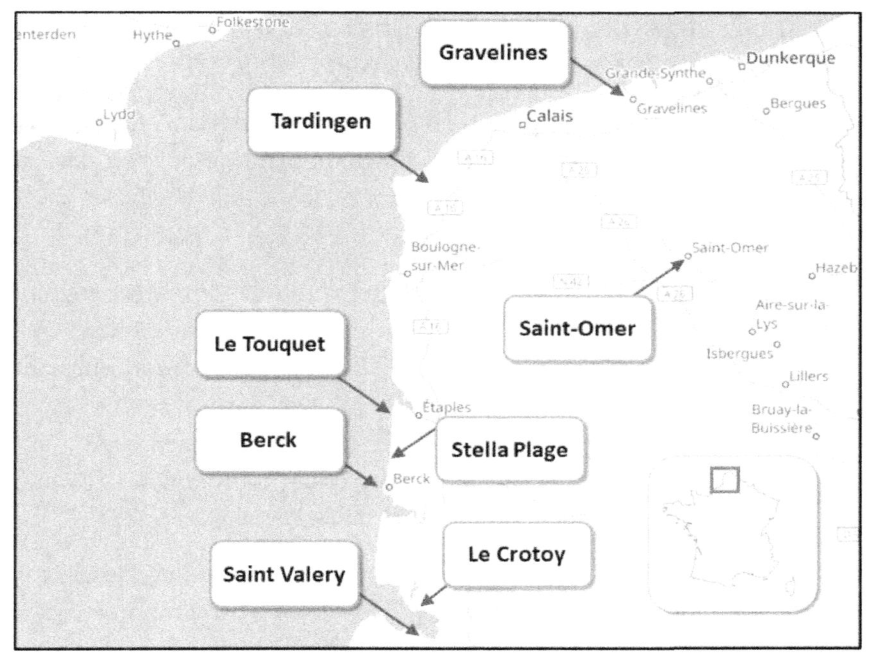

The far north of France

As the ferries and tunnel arrive at Calais or Dunkirk, our first stopovers were in the area to the east and west. **Gravelines**, connected to the North Sea via a canal, is only 16 miles east of Calais, about a 35-minute drive on the free A16 motorway. It has three aires, two close to the town centre and one closer to the beach. We stayed in the aire by the river (GPS: N50.9881, E2.12249).

For a stay in the countryside, the Ferme de l'Horloge near the village of **Tardingen**, within the beautiful Grand Site des Deux-Caps, offers great views over the channel to the English coastline (GPS: N50.85612 E1.65117). Bring your levelling ramps though, the fields are generally sloping, and we suggest arriving in daylight as the roads leading to the farm are smaller country B roads.

Further to the south is a collection of seaside resorts which were traditionally summer escapes for well-heeled Parisians, but these days have a slightly faded air, especially out of season. **Le Touquet-Paris-Plage** west of Étaples is the most obvious of these, easily accessible from l'Hôtellerie de Plein Air Stoneham campsite (closed in winter, GPS:

N50.51092, E1.58875) or the town's two all-year motorhome aires. We stayed in the aire by the nautical centre (GPS: N50.535801, E1.5931).

Further south, **Le Crotoy** on the tidal Baie de Somme has a nice feel and a good selection of restaurants and cafés. The town has several campsites and two motorhome aires, the closest of which is on the Avenue du Château d'Eau by the sea (GPS: N50.21927, E1.63446).

On the southern side of the bay, facing Le Crotoy, is another easy-going resort at **Saint Valery Sur Somme** with its long water-side boardwalk. The town has two campsites and a well laid-out paid motorhome aire with two service points and electrical hook-up available (GPS: N50.18261, E1.62918). If you want to see seals flowing past on the tide in the bay, a short drive from Saint Valery to Le Hourdel is worthwhile. The village has a free basic aire too (GPS: N50.21459, E1.55323).

The best place we found for seal-spotting though was at **Berck-Sur-Mer**, where the *phoques* (grey and common seals) pull themselves in numbers onto the muddy sand at the Bay of Authie at low tide. The town itself isn't particularly enticing but has an aire a short walk from the bay near the lighthouse, the Phare de Berck (GPS: N50.39664, E1.56391).

Seals at low tide at Berck

If you're looking for something (much) quieter with direct access to sand dunes facing out onto *La Manche* (the English Channel), then **Stella Plage** might be for you. This custom-built resort has a few shops and restaurants but, out of season, is practically deserted. The miles-long beach is wind swept and popular with land yachts and surfers. The resort has a free motorhome aire (GPS: N50.47412, E1.57727) protected from the wind by high dunes and several campsites, the closest to the beach being Camping de la Mer, open from April to September (*www.campingdelamer.com*, GPS: N50.472748, E1.577235).

Sand dunes adjacent to the free aire at Stella Plage, on the Opal Coast

If you're travelling with a pet, you'll need to visit a vet before returning to the UK. There's more information about the Animal Health Certificate (AHC) later in the book, but while we're looking at this area of France we used and can recommend an English-speaking vet in **Saint Omer** for several years (Clinique Vétérinaire du Haut Pont, GPS: N50.756196, E2.259491). There's an aire for parking only a short walk from this vet's premises (GPS: N50.756196, E2.259491), or we usually find a free space on the river by the Quai du Commerce (around GPS: N50.754127, E2.262090).

Most recently (in 2024) we stayed at Camping du Fort Lapin in **Calais**, located right alongside the dunes a mile or so from the centre of the city. We were amazed at how much the seafront has changed in the past few years. A €100m investment has created a cutting-edge, activity-based promenade complete with a jaw-dropping 12m-high fire-breathing dragon which stalks the seafront carry passengers daily. All public transport in Calais is free, and there's a bus stop right outside the campsite entrance.

Normandy

Many of us know Normandy as the location of the D-Day landings, *Jour J* in French. Today the coastal areas and inland towns and cities are rich with reminders of this historic event and the days which followed. High quality museums bring the past to life, while endless crosses in moving military cemeteries remind us of the enormous bravery and suffering involved.

The Normandy American Cemetery

We won't try to run through all the locations for visiting the D-Day beaches and museums in this book. The Normandy Tourism website has a very useful (free to download) map and carries lots of information in English (*en.normandie-tourisme.fr*). Instead, here are just a handful of well-known D-Day locations with, where applicable, ideas for overnight stopovers:

- **Arromanches** is the Gold Beach location of prefabricated concrete Mulberry Harbours towed from Britain, sections of which are still visible today. Arromanches has two motorhome aires a short walk from the beach, the Arromanches 360° cinema and other museums. The Les Bas Carreaux campsite is 500m from the town and is open from May to September (*campinglesbascarreaux.com*).
- **Pointe du Hoc** is famous for a daring and deadly assault on cliff-top bunkers and machine gun posts by US Army Rangers. Daytime

parking is available near the site itself (GPS: N49.391983, W0.990248). For the night (or if you're happy to walk or cycle), there are campsites and an aire about 3 miles away in Grandcamp-Maisy, or another site further away at Vierville-sur-Mer.

- The **Normandy American Cemetery** holds the graves of 9,386 military dead (*www.abmc.gov/normandy*). It's sited on a cliff overlooking Omaha Beach and the English Channel, east of St. Laurent-sur-Mer. There's free daytime parking at the cemetery (GPS: N49.356691, W0.851699). For nearby overnight stops, there's an aire and two campsites near Sainte-Honorine-des-Pertes, about 3 miles away.
- **Pegasus Bridge** northeast of Caen was a strategic canal crossing point which the British Airborne Corps attacked and captured early on D-Day, after landing nearby in gliders. The original bridge has been moved to a memorial site a short distance away with free day parking (GPS: N49.243284, W0.271814). Camping des Capucines at Longueville is a 10-minute walk from the bridge (GPS: N49.237853, W0.257255).
- The **Mémorial de Caen** is a memorial and museum located on the outskirts of Caen. It isn't dedicated to D-Day, but instead relays the story of the Battle for Caen in the aftermath of the beach landings. In a wider context it covers WW2 and conflict in the 20th century. You can stay overnight directly outside the memorial at a Camping-Car Park aire (GPS: N49.199257, W0.385789). There's also free daytime parking alongside the aire at the memorial if you want to move on for the evening.

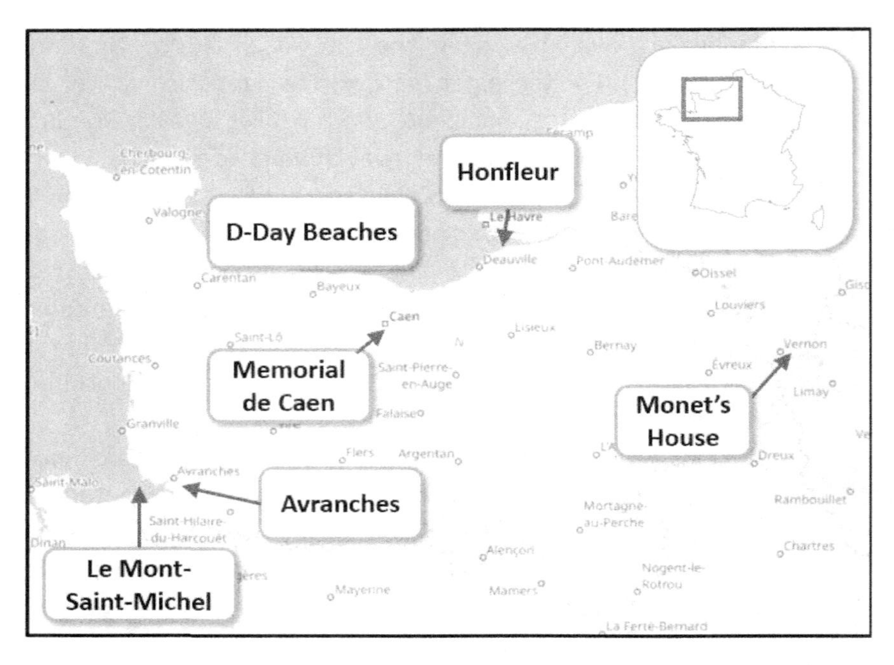

Away from the military memorials and museums, perhaps Normandy's most iconic sight is **Le Mont-Saint-Michel**. The tidal island has an incredibly scenic abbey, connected to the mainland with a bridge constructed in 2014. With over 3 million visitors a year, the island is a little touristy inside, with a gauntlet of souvenir shops as you enter but things calm down as you climb higher. Camping du Mont Saint-Michel is around 2 miles away with a free shuttle bus (*www.camping-montsaintmichel.com*, open April to early October). Just a little further away there's an aire which is open all year, again with access to the free shuttle bus (GPS: N48.608405, W1.508161). Dogs aren't allowed on the buses.

Le-Mont-Saint-Michel

Honfleur was an important trading port in the middle ages, and today is famous for its picturesque *Vieux Bassin*, the old port, undamaged by the ravages of WW2. A UNESCO World Heritage site, the old town is very attractive and well worth a visit. Just be aware that during the summer every man, woman and their dogs will be visiting too! The restaurants surrounding the old quayside are packed, so make sure you get a table and order your *plateau de fruits de mer* or *crêpes* early!

The Vieux Bassin, Honfleur

Honfleur has a huge aire large enough for over 200 motorhomes (it still gets full), just a short walk from the old town (GPS: N49.419255, E0.241534). If you fancy a campsite, Camping Du Phare also has a good central location (*www.normandie-sur-mer.fr/en*).

In the east of Normandy, Claude **Monet's House** (and gardens, complete with lily ponds) is a place of artistic pilgrimage. With around half a million visitors a year, the house is Normandy's second-most visited attraction (after Le Mont-Saint-Michel), so booking in advance might be a good idea. Monet lived and painted here for 43 years up to his death in 1926, after which the house fell into disrepair. It was restored in the 1970s with around US$7m from American donors (*giverny.org*). The house offers free overnight motorhome parking a five-minute walk away (GPS: N49.073221, E1.529853).

Avranches sits on a hill above the Mont-Saint-Michel bay in Western Normandy. It has a rich history, including being the location where the king of England, Henry II, did penance after the murder of Thomas Becket in 1172. More recent history caught our eyes in Patton Square, where a tank stands alongside a stone monument to General Patton's US army who liberated Avranches in August 1944. The town has a free motorhome aire about a 10-minute walk from the Saint-Gervais Basilica (GPS: N48.68674, W1.36816).

Patton Square, a monument to the US Army in Avranches

Brittany

Each part of France enjoys its own regional identity, but perhaps none more so than Brittany. Shops everywhere across *Bretagne* sell the classic Breton striped clothes, jars of salted caramel, fish soups and butter biscuits, all locally produced. Industry is restricted to the larger ports. Almost all of Brittany is an unspoiled paradise of sandy beaches, high cliffs, fields and woods. Villages and towns are filled with quaint houses, cafés and restaurants solidly constructed from local granite.

A cove near Morgat, Crozon Peninsular, Brittany

We've toured Brittany twice. First many moons ago in our campervan, taking the ferry to St Malo with friends, who stayed alongside us in their tent on campsites. Recently we went back in our motorhome, this time travelling to Calais and taking the toll roads (and the impressive Pont du Normandie bridge) across France. Next time we'll use a Brittany Ferries route again, to St Malo or Roscoff to avoid those long drives.

If you choose to use Brittany Ferries, it's worth asking whether anyone you know (in person or on an internet forum for example) is a member of their Club Voyage. If they are, they may be happy to give you a discount code which knocks 10% off your ferry cost (and they get £10 credited to their own ferries).

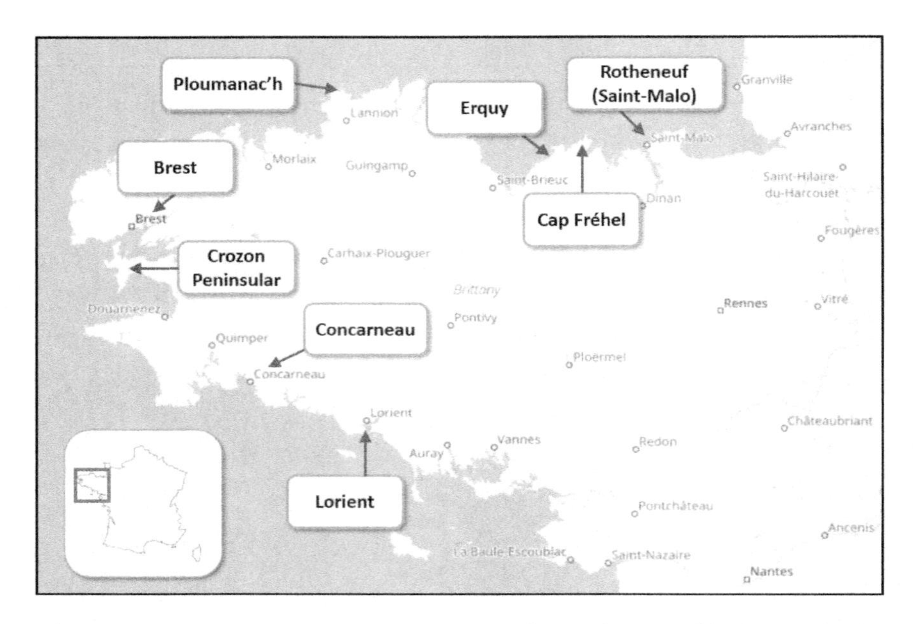

Like many ports across Europe, **Saint-Malo** is often swiftly bypassed by new arrivals on the continent. Although heavily damaged during WW2, the ramparts and the streets of narrow houses were rebuilt between 1948 and 1960. The port, the forts and beaches now make for a pleasant day's wandering.

Saint-Malo, Brittany

You can stay overnight at Saint-Malo's park-n-ride (GPS: N48.643450, W1.993872). This includes the bus into the city (no dogs unless they fit in a carrier). We opted to stay at a very pleasant spot in **Rothenuef**, at Aire Camping-Cars Des Ilots (GPS: N48.68054, W1.96357). Again low-cost, this was an ex-campsite, converted into an aire and within easy driving distance of Saint-Malo and with good bus links. Rothenuef is very pleasant in its own right, with shops, restaurants, rocky headlands and sandy beaches in easy walking distance.

The municipal campsite on the Côtes-d'Armor near **Cap Fréhel** is a relaxed affair set on an expanse of grass with no marked-out spaces. The low-cost site is just the other side of a quiet road from a sandy bay (GPS: N48.664016, W2.341637).

The municipal campsite at Cap Fréhel, Brittany, France

The GR34 long distance 'customs path', which meanders 2,000km around Brittany's coast, runs right past the site entrance. For more on France's Grande Randonnée, or GR, footpaths, see *www.gr-infos.com*. You can either take a cycle path or the GR34 (which takes to the cliff tops on this stretch) through heather and gorse to the lighthouse located on the cape itself. Two and a half miles further around the coast brings you to the impressive sea-facing Fort la Latte.

The charming port of **Erquy** was ablaze with excitement during our stay, with thousands of spectators shouting and admonishing raft racers in the clear waters of the port. We passed through in September and the sun shone throughout, a piece of luck for us as Brittany has a reputation for wet and windy weather.

A very popular raft race in Erquy, Brittany

Erquy has a low-cost motorhome aire facing the sea, a minute's walk from the beach and a 30-minute stroll to the old port (GPS: N48.621399, W2.47231). While we were there, we donned wetsuits, masks and snorkels, and friends took us out foraging for oysters and mussels, which grow wild on the rocks of Cap d'Erquy.

Oysters collected and prepared by fellow motorhomers

Brittany is famous for its pink granite coast, the *Côte de Granite Rose*. It stretches for more than thirty kilometres from Plestin-les-Grèves to Louannec, but we opted to walk a short (and spectacular) section of it around Saint-Guirec and **Ploumanac'h**. We stayed nearby for a couple of nights at the aire in Trégastel (GPS: N48.824221, W3.498769).

Camping Tourony is also well-placed for the same coastal walk (*www.camping-tourony.com*). Alternatively, if you fancy a bit of 5-star luxury, Camping Sandaya Le Ranolien is right on the coastal path (*www.sandaya.fr/nos-campings/le-ranolien*).

Looking across the pink granite rocks to Phare de Mean Ruz

We reached the granite coast from the aire by walking over a stone dam which once held back seawater for two water mills. On our way back the *Patrouille de France* (the French equivalent of the Red Arrows) had us craning our necks at the acrobatics. You can see the *Patrouille's* upcoming schedule on their website (*air.defense.gouv.fr*).

One of the many aquariums at Océanopolis, Brest

The port city of **Brest** in the Finistère department in Brittany was heavily damaged in WW2, so not much of the old centre remains. Our interest in the city lay to the east at the Océanopolis marine wildlife centre (*www.oceanopolis.com*). We spent a good five hours exploring the site's 76 aquariums and pools housing 10,000 animals.

Free overnight motorhome parking is provided right by the Océanopolis entrance, well maintained and set by the pleasure marina (GPS: N48.388842, W4.435510). The parking is barriered off at night, and we stayed a pleasant couple of nights. Another British couple were staying for 10 days, supporting their athlete son who was practicing windfoiling nearby, hoping to make the next summer Olympics. There are no services at the parking area, but there are two service points an 800m drive away (GPS: N48.393309, W4.434750). Brest's botanical gardens are about a mile walk or cycle away. It's free to walk the paths, with a small charge if you choose to visit the greenhouses.

Paris, Île de France

Having long followed the general advice to 'avoid Paris' when driving across France, we eventually bit the bullet when our Australian friends flew in on their way home after walking the Camino de Santiago in Spain.

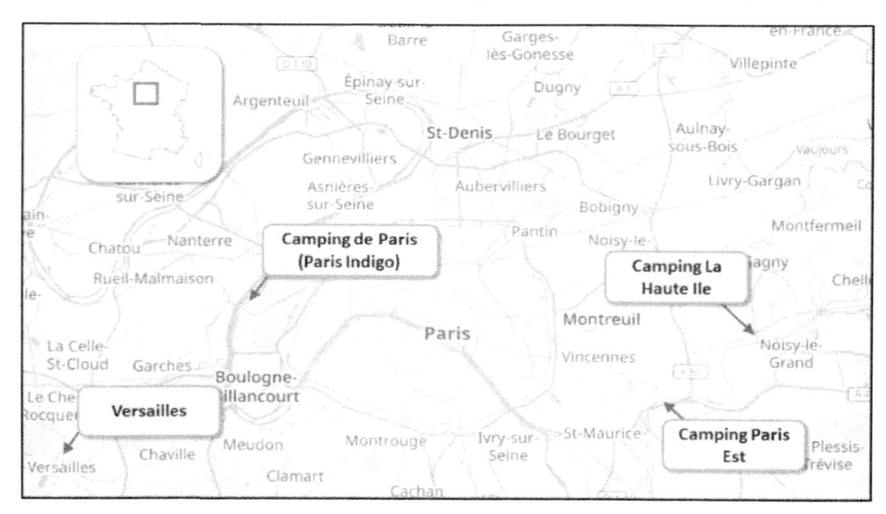

In our research we found that **Paris** is served by at least three, relatively central campsites:

- **Camping de Paris** (*www.campingparis.fr*) to the west, alongside the Bois de Bolougne city park (GPS: N48.86949, E2.23577).
- **Camping Paris Est** (*www.paris-camping.fr*) to the east (GPS: N48.8279583, E2.4771306).
- **Camping La Haute Ile** (*www.neuillysurmarne.fr/votre-ville/decouvrir-neuilly/camping-de-la-haute-ile*) is a municipal site in Neuilly-sur-Marne. While being a little further from Paris than the other two, it's currently the cheapest option for visiting Paris by motorhome (GPS: N48.8538988, E2.541338).

All the campsites are connected to central Paris by public transport, using nearby buses to connect to the *Réseau Express Régional* (the RER, *parisbytrain.com/paris-rer*), which is the Paris underground. The RER stations are also accessible on foot if you're able to walk a few miles.

We stayed at Camping de Paris to the west of the city. As we drove to it we experienced some stop-start traffic, but the motorway generally flowed freely. We accessed the campsite by driving along the D7 dual carriageway, to the north side of the Seine. We missed the turn-off for the bridge, so carried on to the next one, crossing the river and driving north up the D1, finding the campsite on our left marked by flags. The journey in and out was much easier than we'd anticipated. We also noticed that traffic in and around Paris was lightest on a Sunday, when the access roads were almost devoid of traffic.

The Paris CRIT'Air zone, which only used to cover the area of Paris inside the E15 ring road, has now been expanded to cover the surrounding areas, including Camping de Paris and Camping Paris Est (this is the Grand Paris ZFE). This means older motorhomes without a CRIT'Air vignette E, 1, 2 or 3 will not be able to drive to and from these sites (without risking a fine) between 8am and 8pm, Monday to Friday. From January 2025 vehicles with Level 2 vignettes or worse will be affected. For full details and the latest situation check *urbanaccessregulations.eu*.

The Eiffel Tower, Paris

While we were staying in Paris, we opted to use public transport to get from Camping de Paris to Versailles, to visit the opulent palace and gardens there. To do this we walked to Suresnes and took the train to Versailles. Other options would have been:

- Drive to Versailles and stay at the Huttopia Campsite (*europe.huttopia.com*, GPS: N48.7942728, E2.1609574) or use one of the parking locations on *park4night.com*.
- Find a parking area or campsite further outside Paris and Versailles and take the train into the city.

If you're planning to visit Disneyland Paris (*www.disneylandparis.com*), to the east of the city, the park has paid overnight motorhome parking (GPS: N48.877346, E2.786208). It's a basic parking area with limited facilities (no electricity, but there are showers and toilets) and is expensive (€40 a night). If you plan to stay a few nights, it's worth checking whether buying an annual pass (one which includes parking) would be cost-effective. This reduces the cost of parking to €15 a night. You can buy the passes by calling Disneyland before leaving the UK.

Grand Est

The vineyards of Champagne lie to the east of Paris, around Reims, Épernay, Bouzy and Troyes. If you're a wine buff you can really go to town visiting a string of Champagne houses including the big and famous ones like Moët & Chandon and Pol Roger in Épernay, or Veuve Cliquot and Champagne Mumm in Reims. We were surprised to find there are around 260 champagne houses in total, as well as the big names there are lots of smaller ones in this area, some of which are very welcoming to motorhomes. Even if you've no interest in the fizz, the rolling vineyards which blanket the hills surrounding over 300 villages present lovely vistas in summer and autumn, although the vines are a little less attractive as leaf-less stumps in winter!

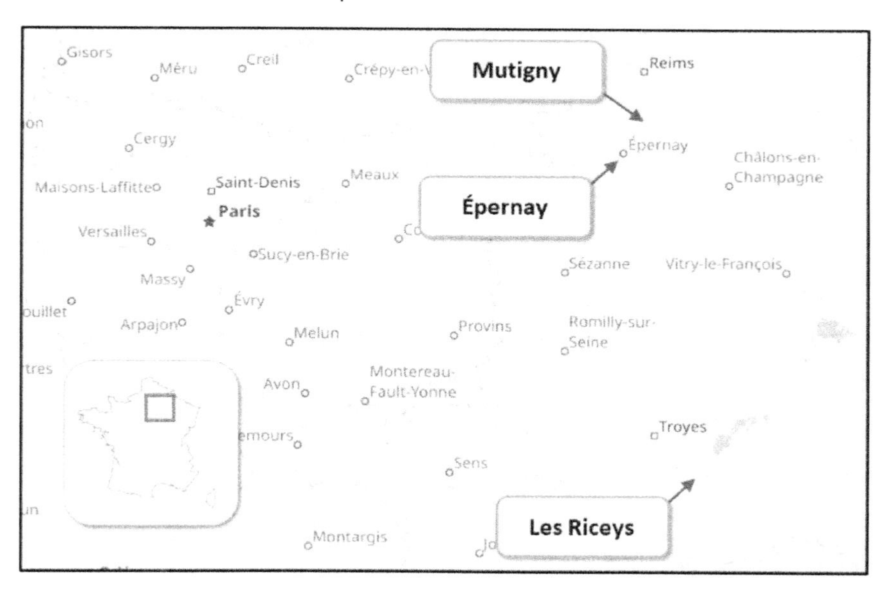

We haven't explored the Champagne region in any depth, but we have enjoyed a few nights here over the years. Starting in the south, we decided to visit one of the smaller houses which offers tastings and motorhome overnight stays under the France Passion scheme. Arriving at Champagne Pascal Walczak (*www.champagne-walczak.fr*) in **Les Riceys**, a lady appeared as we pulled up in the car park and welcomed us in French, showing us where we could stay for the night (GPS: N47.994202, E4.362300).

Being complete Champagne novices, we should have done some research before knocking on the door for a tasting. Thankfully the very well-spoken lady presenting the wines kindly put up with our terrible language and lack of tasting knowledge and we escaped clutching a bottle of Champagne and laughing! A little embarrassed we opted not to stay the night, but we could have slept there, giving us two glasses of Champagne (in the tasting room), the bottle we bought and a night's pitch for a total cost of €15.20 (around £13.50). Pretty good value, although this was a few years ago now!

Champagne tasting at Champagne Pascal Walczak

In **Épernay** we had a completely different experience. We arrived in the town to find the small motorhome aire had been expanded to cater for about 30 to 40 motorhomes. Well, sort of. An additional area on a basketball court had been provided for an English tour company, although it was full of French-registered motorhomes. When we looked the tour company up, they'd gone out of business, so like our French neighbours, we opted to wing it and stayed there. The reason for all of this? The *Habits de Lumière* annual festival was taking place, which was free to visit, and we can highly recommend it. The festival takes place in December on the kilometre-long Avenue de Champagne. If you aren't there for the festival, you can still visit the famous Champagne houses and tour their cellars.

The aire is about 2km from the centre of the town (GPS: N49.036098, E3.951430), or if you want to camp instead, the municipal campsite is open from the end of April to the end of September:

epernay.fr/services-et-demarches/mobilite/camping-cars/camping-municipal

On a more peaceful, bucolic note, we spent a night in the free hilltop aire alongside the village of **Mutigny**, north-east of Épernay (GPS: N49.06915, E4.02686). We visited in July, so the vines were lush with leaves, although the grapes were still hard and small like rounded bullets. The village was quiet but had a self-guided walk around it taking in a couple of Champagne houses offering tastings (alternatively you could pay for a 90-minute tour).

Lush green vineyards around Mutigny in July

Centre-Val de Loire

Famous for its magnificent collection of Renaissance-period châteaux, the meandering Loire River is very welcoming to motorhome tourists, with many campsites and aires within striking distance of the big attractions like Chambord and Chenonceau.

Starting away from the châteaux, we used our usual 'visiting a city by motorhome' approach for going to see **Orléans**, staying outside the city and travelling in on public transport. This works well for us as it means we avoid the stress of driving into a city, and unless we can find secure parking in the city itself, we feel safer leaving the van somewhere further away. This time we stayed in a free aire by a park in the small town of **Saran** (GPS: N47.95128, E1.87327) and took a 20-minute bus into the city to explore, then got the bus back out again in the evening.

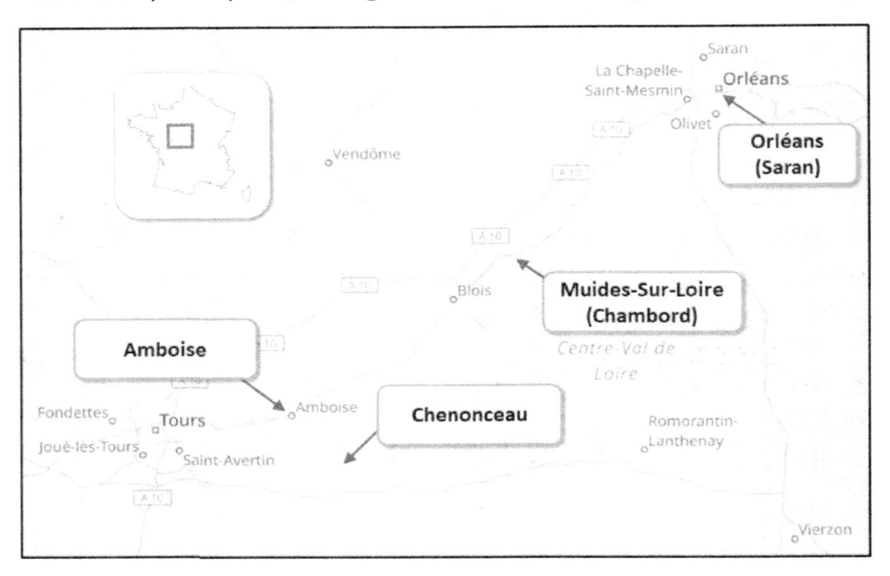

We'll be honest and tell you now, we've only been inside one of the Loire châteaux, the one at **Chenonceau**. The château provides daytime parking for motorhomes in the main car park and there is a free aire a short stroll away for overnight stays (GPS: N47.33051, E1.06861). It's by a train line, but the location made the occasional noise worthwhile.

Chenonceau and its gardens in October

Château Chambord has a large motorhome aire in its grounds. While you have to pay to stay in the aire and there is no service point, the location is fantastic (GPS: N47.619157, E1.510954). As we were visiting friends and staying on the Camping Les Château des Marais campsite at **Muides-sur-Loire**, we didn't use the aire. The campsite is a short walk from the Loire, and about a 4-mile cycle ride from the château. The campsite accepts the ACSI CampingCard for discounted out-of-season stays (GPS: N47.665826, E1.528656).

Château Chambord

At **Amboise** we stayed at the municipal campsite (*www.camping-amboise.com*, GPS: N47.41742, E0.98956), which is open from March to October (there is also a motorhome aire next to it which is open all year). This low-cost site is a short walk from the bridge over the Loire into the town and to the château, the resting place of Leonardo de Vinci.

The town has a weekly market on a Tuesday morning between around 9am and 1pm, with lots of delicious fresh produce available.

Château d'Amboise, seen from the campsite side of the Loire

Nouvelle-Aquitaine - The Dordogne

The Dordogne River meanders its way through the ancient region of Périgord, an area which has long attracted British ex-pats. Despite the increased number of British registration plates, this area still has a quintessential French feel to it, with its green wooded hills, butter-coloured cliffs and quaint, affluent, well-kept villages. We can provide only the very barest selection from the plethora of places to stay in this part of France.

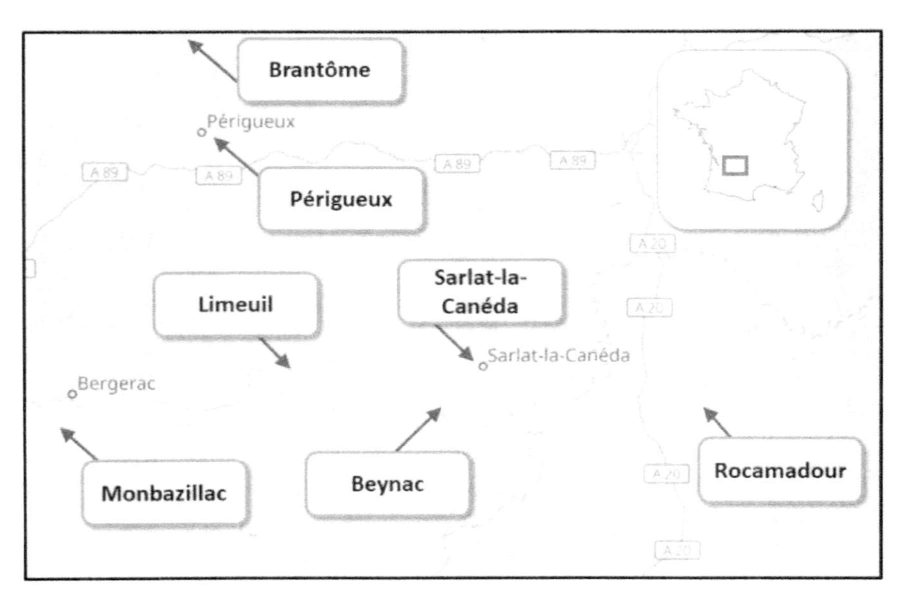

Our first stop is just south of the famous river at **Rocamadour**. If we'd opened our guidebook this pilgrim town built on the side of a gorge, would be certain to feature. As it was, we were visiting friends who live in France and pointed it out to us. There are several parking places above the town, all of which are likely to be busy in season. We stayed in the official aire by Parking P2 (GPS: N44.800042, E1.615397).

Beynac-et-Cazenac is nestled between the Dordogne and a cliff-face, which is itself topped by a château. It's highly photogenic, especially in the late evening when it basks in the glow of the setting sun. The château parking was the first place we 'wild camped' in France, very nervously, despite the fact we were in such a quiet location. We've since found out it's now the aire for the town (GPS: N44.844923, E1.145777).

Beynac, Dordogne

At **Limeuil** we found ourselves squeezing under a bridge onto a grassy motorhome parking area on the banks of the Vezere just before it flows into the Dordogne (GPS: N44.882396, E0.890952). The small size of the village might explain why it has a much less 'touristy' feel than some of the others on the river. We enjoyed wandering the picturesque streets and collecting walnuts fallen from trees alongside the river. In warmer months we'd have been tempted by the village's river beach too.

Further to the west, south of Bergerac and again away from the river lies the dessert wine commune of **Monbazillac**. We've a vivid memory of a family of wild boar crossing the road in size order as we drove through the vines towards a very popular (almost legendary, it seems) France Passion site at Domaine de La Lande (GPS: N44.788220, E0.495899). The owner of the vineyard, a fellow motorhome-traveller, sells all his wine to visitors to his aire. We really enjoyed our night by the vines, chatting as best we could with the owner in our broken French!

A night by the vines at Domaine de la Lande, Monbazillac

North of the Dordogne lie some of the region's most idyllic villages, imposing castles and historic caves. **Brantôme** has earned its place in France's *Les Plus Beaux Détours* with its atmospheric river-side Benedictine Abbey. The abbey and town are both easily accessible from the motorhome aire (GPS: N45.360500, E0.648312).

Abbey of Brantôme

South of Brantôme lies **Périgueux**, a city with Roman remains including an amphitheatre and villa. Archaeology aside, we found Périgueux to be a very attractive city to visit with its narrow medieval alleys, towering cathedral and a host of chocolate and pastry shops which threaten to expand your waistline at every turn! We enjoyed a quiet stay in the town's aire near the river (GPS: N45.18762, E0.73097).

Last but by no means least, **Sarlat le Canéda** is perhaps the region's most famous town. Wonderfully restored medieval and renaissance buildings crowd around you, their yellow stone walls seeming to glow on a sunny afternoon. There's plenty to see, ask at the tourist office for help, but be aware you'll most likely be sharing the sights with a small horde of fellow tourists. The town has an aire which is a little derided by French *camping-caristes* for being too expensive, but it is conveniently close to the centre (GPS: N44.8955, E1.212573).

We shouldn't leave this area without at least mentioning the region's famous caves. Although the closest we got to them was driving past troglodyte houses cut into the rock, there are some magnificent *grottes* to be explored if the underground world draws you. The most famous is Lascaux, with its walls covered in prehistoric art. The original cave has been closed to the public for over 50 years due to the damage caused by the presence of hundreds of visitors per day.

Impressive replicas have since been created, including the modern visitor complex at Lascaux IV opened in 2016. You can park for the day in Parking 2 at Lascaux IV (GPS: N45.053919, E1.167651), or stay in the campsite or aire at Montignac and walk or cycle a couple of miles to the site.

Nouvelle-Aquitaine - Atlantic Coast

When we think of the French Atlantic Coast, these things come to mind: sand, sunshine, pine trees, surf, oysters and bucolic islands with their salt flats and beaches. There are, of course, also the vines and wines around Bordeaux, although in our travels we've somehow managed to bypass them, perhaps in too much of a hurry to head south to Spain for winter sunshine. The area to the far south-west of France forms part of the historical Basque country, which straddles both sides of the Spanish border. You might spot some signs of this influence on local culture, such as multi-lingual road signs and *pelota* courts.

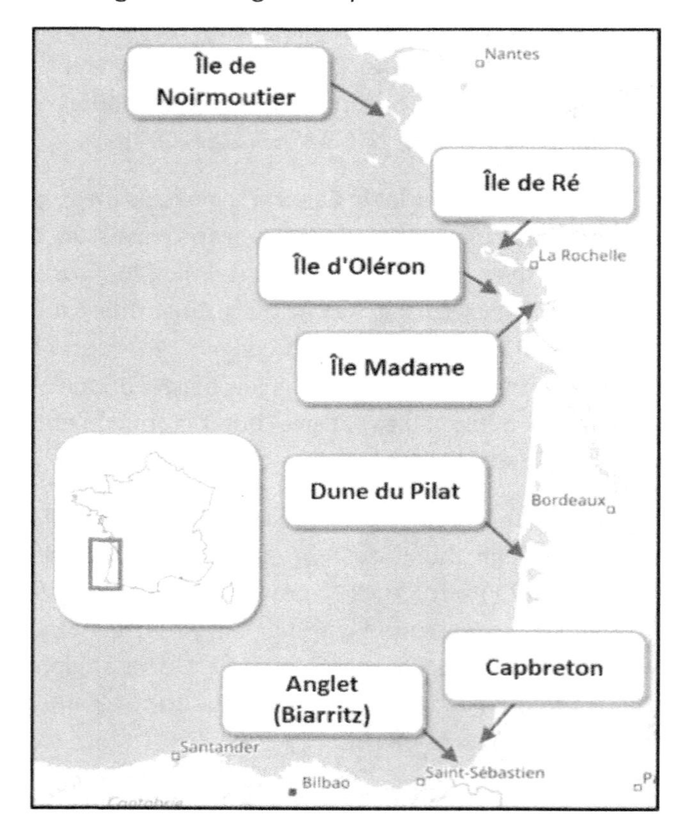

Starting in the south, we've a couple of favourite aires on the route down to Spain. The aire alongside the sea near **Anglet** is set inside a hedged area above the beach, where countless surfers bob around waiting for waves (GPS: N43.50635, W1.5349). There's a promenade along the beach which you can use to stroll to Biarritz in about 40 minutes (Biarritz has an aire of its own if you want a shorter walk). Or you can just opt to wander around Anglet, doing some shopping or chilling out on the sand. The Anglet aire is low-cost and has lots of space, so it's popular with larger units towing trailers. If you prefer campsites, there's a very good choice in this part of the world.

Looking south towards Biarritz and the Pyrenees from the aire near Anglet

A little further north, the aire at **Capbreton** is a personal favourite, although it's a somewhat rambling affair (GPS: N43.63672, W1.44721). The aire is a large parking area set back from the rolling Atlantic waves by sand dunes, with electrical hook-up in. We enjoy the surfer-vibe of the place, and usually take a 40-minute stroll (or 10-minute bike ride) into the town to eyeball the fish market and eat an ice cream. Again, there are plenty of campsites if you prefer.

Climbing the Dune du Pilat

To the south-west of Bordeaux, just south of Pyla-sur-Mer, you'll find the weird sight and climbing challenge that is the **Dune du Pilat**, Europe's highest sand dune (GPS: N44.589715, W1.215588).

Backed by a pine forest and overlooking the sea, we really enjoyed dragging ourselves up to the top of the dune. You might want to come outside of peak season though. Arriving in August, we crawled for miles past *bouchon* (traffic jam) signs to find the large car parks for the dune were packed, so we scouted out an area by the road we could stay in for a couple of hours. If you wanted to sleep by the dune, there's a series of campsites right up against the base, plus an aire about 2 miles south, set among the trees off the D218 (GPS: N44.557537, E1.238315).

Further north, France's Atlantic islands have been a big draw to us over the years, including:

- **Île d'Oléron** – the largest island on the French Atlantic coast is famed for its oyster farming, sandy beaches and whitewashed fishermen's houses with bright blue or green shutters. We enjoyed several nights on the island, staying at France Passion, aire and campsite locations.
- **Île de Ré** - in one of our early campervan forays we took the arching toll bridge over to this island from La Rochelle (which is itself well worth a visit, and has its own collection of aires and campsites).
- **Île de Noirmoutier** - there's a free bridge to this popular island, as well as a causeway which floods at high tide (there are lots of warning signs). The island has several campsites and aires, large areas of salt-producing pools, oyster beds and 25 miles of beaches.
- **Île Madame -** we visited this tiny island for the novelty factor, if we're honest. It's only accessible at low tide along a causeway, which caused us a few moments of doubt! There is an inexpensive campsite on the island (Camping La Ferme Aquacole, GPS: N45.95990, W1.11622), which would make a great place for anyone wanting to really get away from it all.

The submerged causeway leading to Île de Noirmoutier

Auvergne-Rhône-Alpes - The Alps

The Alps are a favourite area for us, rising from the Mediterranean and sweeping in a giant curve north and then east into Switzerland. They have their own legendary tourist itinerary in the *Route des Grandes Alpes*. This is a (roughly) 450-mile series of roads which run from Lac Léman (Lake Geneva) and south over 18 to 23 mountain passes, depending on which version of the route you follow. Eventually you arrive at the Mediterranean Sea, frazzled and buzzing! The highest passes are only open between around mid-June and October, so time your arrival carefully.

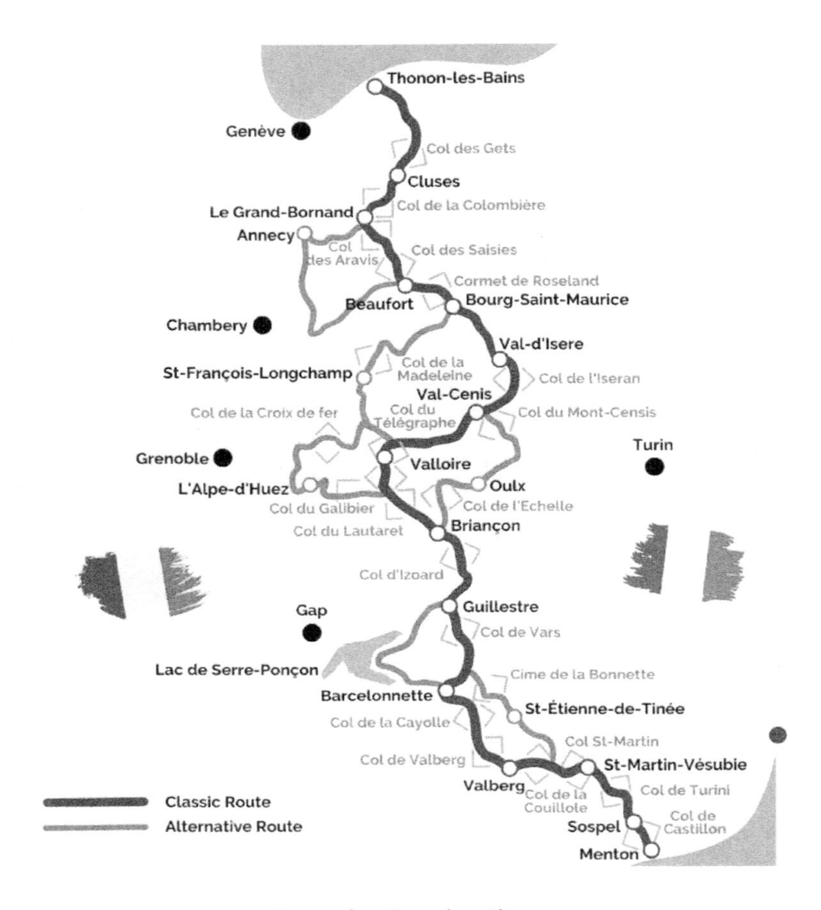

Route des Grandes Alpes

Most of our travels have been outside the ski season, although we have dabbled in winter high altitude travelling to get some experience of it. The Alps are obviously very big hills with some passes over 2,500m above sea level. They present ascents and descents which can exceed 10 miles in length, complete with zig-zagging hairpins, overhanging rocks and tunnels and, from winter into the late spring, potentially long stretches of snow and ice to deal with. Motorhome travellers regularly handle all of these, armed with some basic knowledge and skills which we'll share later in this book.

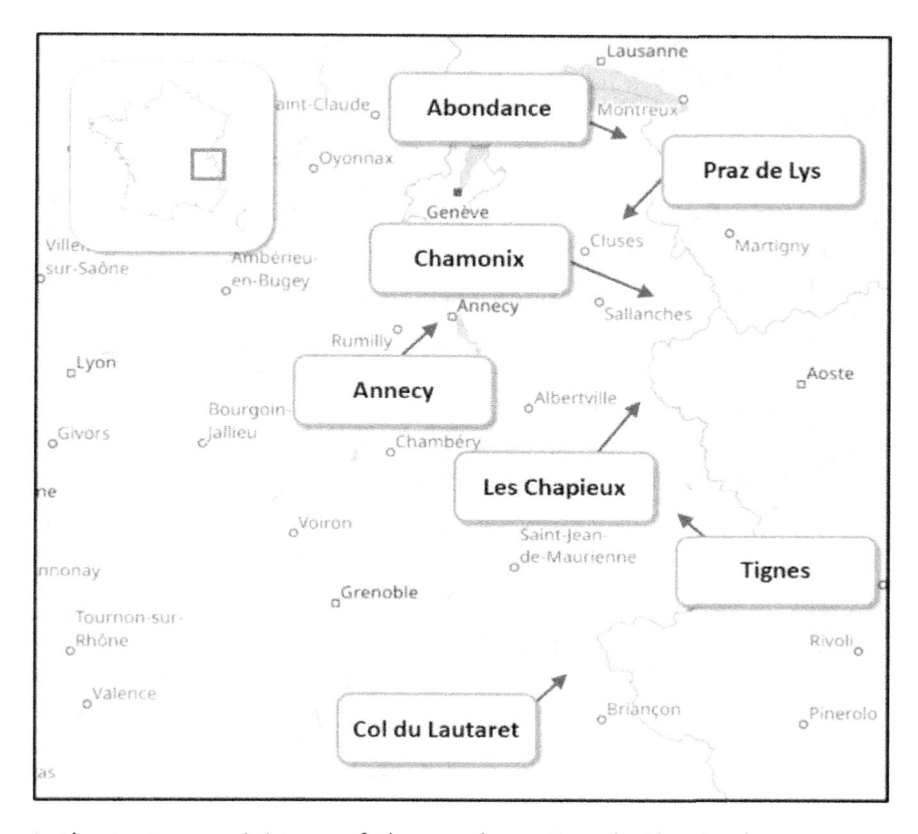

Let's start our mini-tour of the northern French Alps in the gateway town of **Annecy**, south of Geneva. We're not yet in the mountains here, instead there is the picturesque old town, Le Vieil Annecy, laid out beside the River Thiou which flows into the adjacent Lake Annecy. It's a bit of a tourist hot spot, so there are plenty of restaurants and cafés. We've stayed once in the popular free aire alongside the lake (GPS: N45.890684, E6.138802), and once we free-camped above the town besides the basilica as the aire was full (GPS: N45.8928, E6.12701).

Into the mountains now, our first winter experience of a ski resort was at **Le Praz de Lys** in February (GPS: N46.14136, E6.60321). Nervous of driving in the snow, we only had mud and snow tyres fitted (full winter tyres will be mandatory in France during the winter from November 2024), although we had also bought snow chains. We got our chance to give the chains a try after two days in the resort's motorhome aire.

While we were there the night-time temperature dropped to -10°C during a minor blizzard (it was nice and warm inside our van, but we managed to run low on gas by preparing badly!). Although a snow plough cleared most of the parking area each afternoon, we still had to drive up a snow-covered slope to leave. After a friendly French neighbour checked we'd fitted the chains properly to our front wheels we rolled off gingerly and found we had plenty of grip, but we were still overjoyed when we reached the main road which was completely clear of snow.

Le Praz de Lys Motorhome Aire in February

Part of the Route des Grand Alpes, the scenery around the **Col du Lautaret**, which is on the road up to the Col du Galibier, is spectacular. At the Col du Lautaret itself, at 2,058m above sea level, there's an informal summer-only free parking area around which marmots squeal and the distant rumble of motorbike engines echoes (GPS: N45.0325, E6.40758). There are no services here, come full of water with empty waste and loo tanks, but there are restaurants.

The snaking Col du Galibier

Chamonix is one of Europe's major Alpine sports centres, occupying a valley position besides the jaw-dropping Mont Blanc Massif, attracting huge numbers of both winter and summer visitors. We were lucky to be invited to stay on the driveway of a couple who live in the town, but we've also free-camped alongside the road on the exit towards Switzerland (GPS: N45.92827, E6.87674). We wouldn't have needed to do this in summer, as there's a large aire available underneath the double-station Aiguille du Midi cable car (GPS: N45.916263, E6.870050). There are also several campsites in and around Chamonix, mostly in Les Bossons around two miles from the centre. Many of these sites close in winter, but Les 2 Glaciers in Les Bossons stays open from mid-December to mid-November (*www.les2glaciers.com*, GPS: N45.9015, E6.8375).

While you're in Chamonix, we can't recommend the Aiguille du Midi highly enough. It's not a cheap cable car ride, but it takes you right up from Chamonix to 3842m and as close to Mont Blanc as you can get without hiking or climbing. On a clear day the views are breath-taking. The cable car got very busy in summer, attracting long queues, but we got the second car of the day at around 6.30am and walked straight to the ticket office and into the car, with no queues at all.

View from the Aiguille du Midi towards the Italian Alps

Near the border with Switzerland is the Alpine village of **Abondance**. We were staying in the aire (GPS: N46.28017, E6.71506) when we spotted the Fantasticable (*www.fantasticable.com*) a short drive away at Pré-la-Joux near to Châtel. This adrenaline-fuelled attraction consists of two consecutive zipwires along which you fly at up to 60mph, attached with a harness, at up to 240m above the hamlet of Plaine-Dranse. After we'd 'flown', still buzzing we drove back to Abondance and were directed to stay in the ski telecabin car park for the night, as the town's official aire was being used for a classic car show to celebrate Bastille Day.

If you want to really escape the world, then **Les Chapieux** could be for you. This tiny hamlet's part of the Tour du Mont Blanc, a 110 mile walk through Switzerland, Italy and France and one of the country's classic long-distance hiking trails. We restricted ourselves to about 6 miles of the trail, enjoying the valley for its serenity. There's no mobile signal here, but there is an informal parking area in the valley, only available in summer and it comes with a warning that it might flood in wet weather (GPS: N45.69526, E6.73407).

Informal motorhome parking at Les Chapieux

It is easily possible to stay in several of the larger ski resorts in the French Alps, such as **Tignes**. The Col de l'Iseran carried us there after we'd waited for it to open, its sides still metres high with snow and ice even in late June. In Tignes itself we stayed in the parking area a short walk from the cable car station which takes summer skiers up to the Grande Motte glacier (GPS: N45.457947, E6.897960). This parking area isn't accessible to motorhomes in winter. For winter access to ski resorts, websites like *www.winterised.com* are very useful.

Auvergne-Rhône-Alpes - The Vercors Massif

While some of the gorge roads in France might cause the loss of a few of the driver's (and passenger's) hairs, the balcony roads in the Vercors would have you reaching for a *toupée*. Mostly impassable in all but the smallest of campervans, they nevertheless make for wonderful, impressive excursions if you've the energy to cycle, walk or run through them.

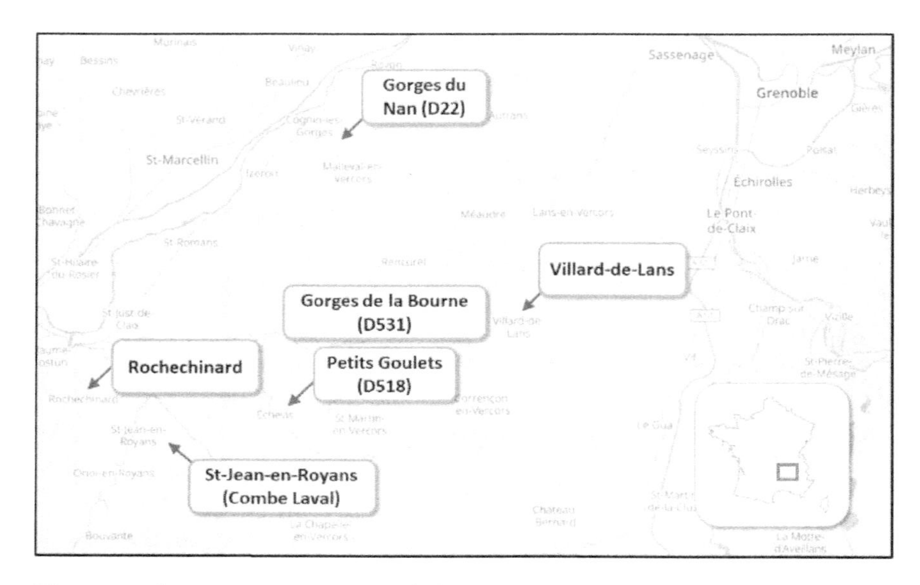

The most impressive section of the **Gorges du Nan** is just a couple of miles up the **D22** from free daytime parking (GPS: N45.170777, E5.412382) or Camping La Chatonnière in Cognin-les-Gorges (GPS: N45.171276, E5.415020). The road bends back and forth a couple of times under trees, nothing special, but suddenly dives left through a tiny tunnel and pops you out high (very high) onto the side of a cliff with fantastic views down into the gorge below.

Gorges du Nan, Vercors, France

The church at **Rochechinard** had lots of five-star reviews in the aires apps and proved to be a relaxing stop-over (GPS: N45.03139, E5.24617), with walks through the surrounding forest to the ruined Château de Rochechinard, impressively perched on a spike of rock.

All alone for the night, free parking by a small church near Rochechinard

Consulting the map, we could see that the famous **Combe Laval** was cyclable from **Saint-Jean-en-Royans**, which has a free motorhome aire (GPS: N45.0202, E5.2905). After enjoying a *menu du jour* in one of the town's restaurants, we cycled up the D76 to the incredible balcony road leading to the Col de la Machine. According to our Michelin map, and the signs at the entrance to the Combe Laval, it was passable in vehicles under 3.5 tonnes and less than 3.5m high, but we really wouldn't recommend driving it in any size of motorhome!

The Combe Laval, Vercors

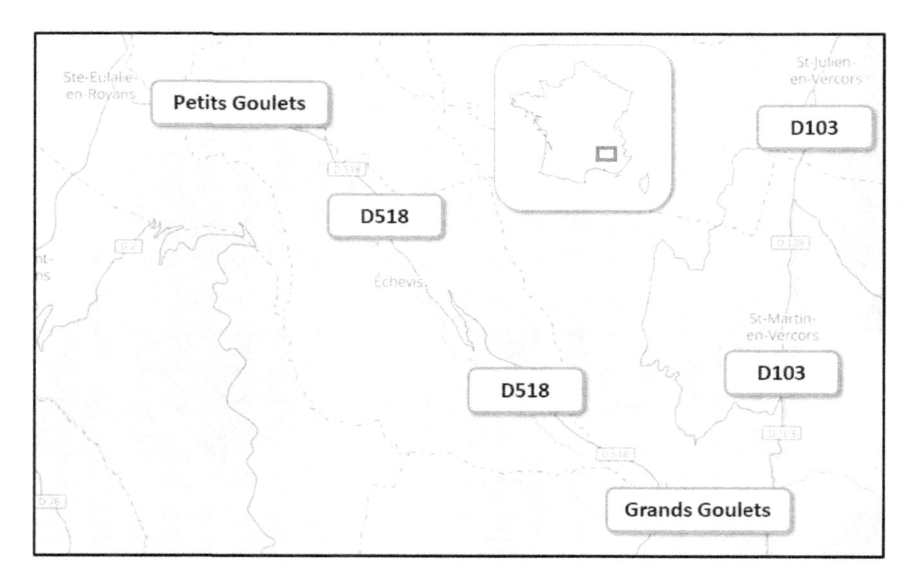

Our research before driving into the Vercors suggested that the D531, the Gorges de la Borne, is both (a) a fantastic road to drive and (b) too narrow for a motorhome to drive comfortably. Not wanting to ramp up stress levels too high, we opted to head east via the tunnels of the **Petits Goulets** instead, the D518. This road used to complete its route east to the D103 via the **Grands Goulets**, another bonkers balcony road, but it had to be closed in 2005 after a series of fatal accidents (you're not even allowed to walk down it now). The D518 uses a tunnel (nice and wide but far from picturesque) these days to reach the D103.

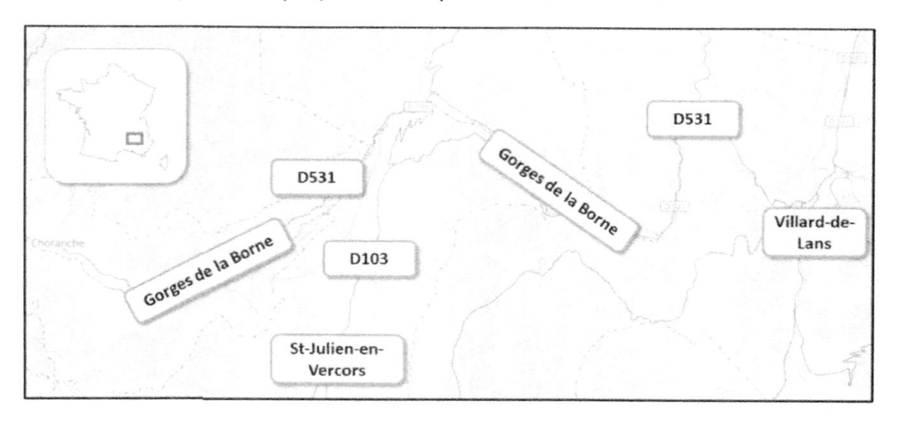

Unfortunately, our next step was to drive north up past Saint-Martin-en-Vercors and **Saint-Julien-en-Vercors** on the D103 to where it meets the D531. Our assumption had been that the **Gorges de la Borne** section of the D531 lay to the west, and we'd get an easy ride down this part of the road to **Villard-de-Lans**. Nope! Turns out the whole of the D531 consists of narrow road, overhangs, small tunnels and lots of tourist traffic. This is a spectacular route and not impassable in a motorhome, but we'd suggest trying to avoid weekends and the busier summer months! Villard-de-Lans proved a pleasant spot to relax, and we stayed for a couple of days in the free aire of the ski resort which remained lively with hikers, even in summer (GPS: N45.06627, E5.55573).

Provence-Alpes-Côte-d'Azur

Peter Mayle made this region of France famous in his best-selling memoir *A Year in Provence*, back in 1989. Peter based his book around his home in Ménerbes, south-east of Avignon, but Provence is a varied region taking in part of the Alps and the Côte d'Azur (French Riviera), as well as deep gorges, meandering rivers, forests and rolling farmlands.

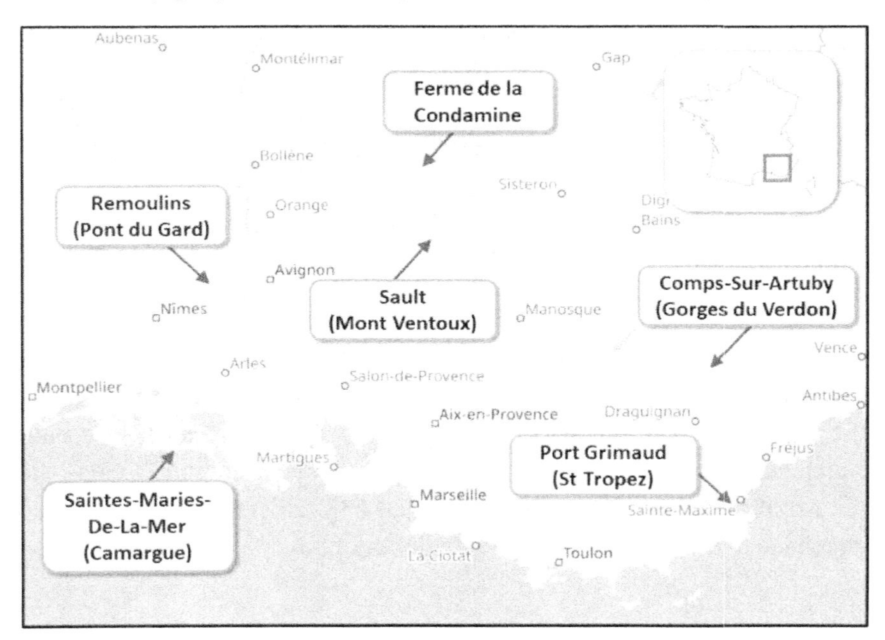

Our first taste of Provence in a motorhome was at the **Pont du Gard**, north-east of the town of Nîmes (which itself has an incredible Roman amphitheatre). A couple had gotten in touch through our *ourtour.co.uk* blog to say they were trying out campervan life and we all decided to meet up at the famous Roman aqueduct. It turned out they'd bought an old ambulance from eBay, fitted it out with a bed and a gas cooker bolted to the top of a sideboard, dubbed it the 'Glambulance' and headed off into Europe! We ended up good friends and later toured Morocco and Switzerland with them - they'd bought a Hymer A Class by that point. Although it's possible to overnight in a motorhome at the Pont du Gard car park, we opted to stay in the aire in the village of **Remoulins**, in walking distance from the aqueduct (a new aire has since been built at GPS: N43.93795, E4.55516).

Pont du Gard

For the ornithologists out there, the name **Camargue** will likely be familiar as an internationally-known wetland. It's also home to a breed of white horses, the Camarguais, and semi-feral fighting bulls, bred for export to Spain. The seaside town of **Saintes-Maries-de-la-Mer** has two campsites and three motorhome aires, clearly a popular base for visiting the Camargue. We stayed in the aire furthest east, close to the path which runs across Digue à la Mer, the sea dyke which cuts across the mouth of the Rhône (GPS: N43.45399, E4.43826). Walking the path, we got to view lots of birdlife, including flocks of pink flamingos.

Flamingos in the Camargue

For a taste of Tour de France legend, we challenged our 20-year-old turbo-less 3.1 tonne motorhome to climb the 1,909m-high **Mont Ventoux**, dubbed the 'Beast of Provence'. With a short rest to cool the engine on the way up, we made it to the top to be treated to a wind-blasted world of snow and rock with 360° views of the Provence countryside. While it is possible to stay the night in a parking area or campsite close to the summit, the wind was blowing a hoolie, so we opted to descend from the mountain along the D164 to the east and stay at a free aire in **Sault** (GPS: N44.094374, E5.413074).

Memorial to Tour de France rider Tom Simpson on Mont Ventoux

One of many lavender fields in Provence

To get a little closer to the locals, you can't beat the France Passion scheme. We opted to head for a Provence lavender farm near, well, nowhere really! The **Ferme de la Condamine** (between Saint-Jalle and Saint-Sauveur-Gouvernet, GPS: N44.32717, E5.33209) has a parking area alongside sun-washed lavender fields and a small shop selling delicious apricots (in season), and other farm produce. The farm even has its own service point, which most France Passion sites don't. The owners were very welcoming, which is very much the norm at France Passion locations.

The **Gorges du Verdon**, Europe's deepest canyon, lies to the south-east of Provence and makes for a memorable driving experience! We started off taking the roads to the north, the D952 to La Palud-sur-Verdon and then south on the D23, along the circular *Route des Crêtes* (*www.verdontourisme.com*, open between March and November).

After several miles, just after Chalet de la Maline, we came across a 'one-way' sign, meaning the anti-clockwise route we were trying to drive wasn't possible. We backtracked 20 or so miles along the D23 and took the roads south of the canyon, the D925 and D71 between Moustiers-Sainte-Marie and **Comps-Sur-Artuby**, where we stayed in a pleasant aire (GPS: N43.705964, E6.506233).

View over the Gorges du Verdon

This is a spectacular drive with incredible views but is narrow with passing places in parts. It would be best avoided on summer weekends, and in our opinion isn't for the faint-hearted (or those with a big rig). We'd suggest you check it out on Google Streetview or search for some photos of the road before having a go at it.

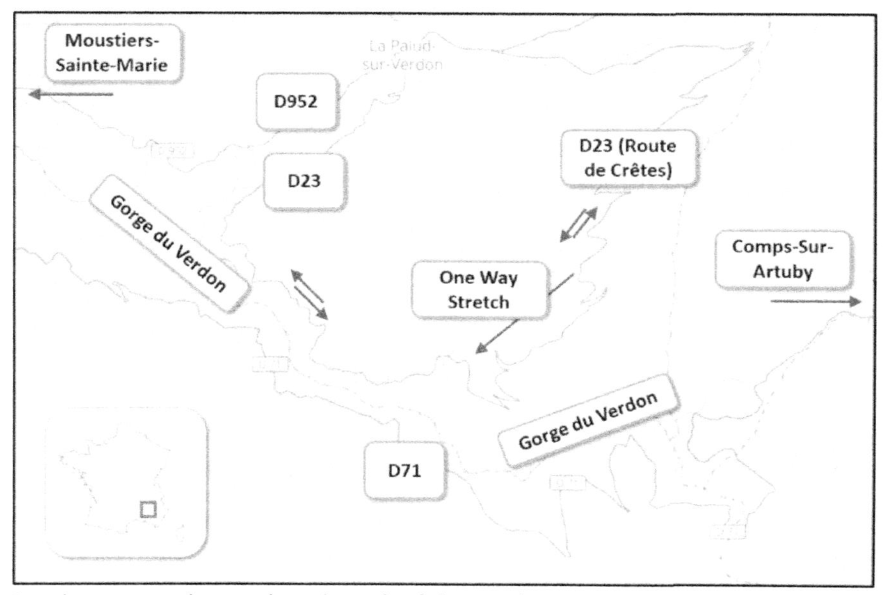

Road routes to the north and south of the Verdon Gorge

Tunnel du Fayet on the D71 south of the Gorges du Verdon

The Mediterranean coastline in Provence can be easily accessed from Lyon using the A7, aptly-named the *Autoroute de Soleil* (the Sun Motorway). We stayed at Camping de la Plage (GPS: N43.280578, E6.586379), just outside **Port Grimaud**, our feet practically in the water on the site's sandy, beachside pitches (we had a bit of a job getting off the sand when we left mind you!). Port Grimaud itself is a fascinating spot, a kind of modern-day Venice, but the big draw must be **Saint-Tropez**, just a short boat ride away and residence for various staggeringly-expensive super yachts.

Occitanie

The Occitane region in the south-west of France played host to our longest break-down yet, keeping us for almost a month once when our clutch gave up. Thankfully we were able to limp around the area while we were waiting for the garage to fit us in after the Easter break. We found the area really interesting, from the big and famous sights like medieval Carcassone and the engineering feat that is the Canal du Midi to small but beautiful spots like the Héric Gorge near Mons.

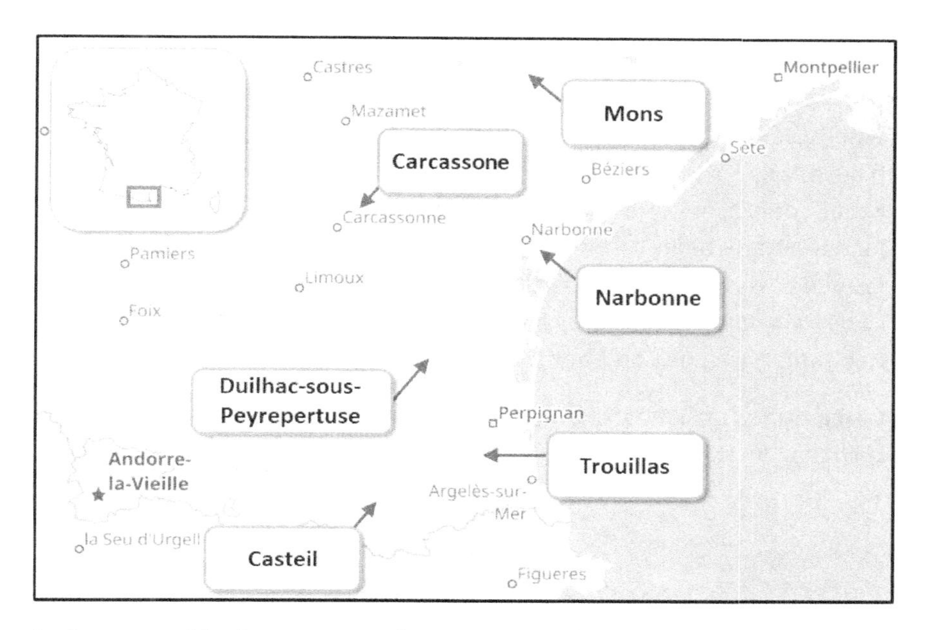

Let's start with that gorge. After our motorhome was finally fixed in Narbonne, we headed north into the Haut-Languedoc Regional Nature Park. We'd got wind of a nice-looking aire near **Mons**, set among woods at the base of the Héric Gorge (*www.minervois-caroux.com*), which is free out of season (GPS: N43.573433, E2.968036). The parking area and gorge looked idyllic and turned out to be just that. We even managed a dip in the crystal-clear waters, although it was a little nippy in April!

Héric Gorge near Mons, Hérault Department (source: Wikipedia)

Narbonne, as well as being the home of the very busy Fiat garage that repaired our clutch, is also a historic Roman town, at one time a port with access to the Mediterranean nine miles away. The town used to have a large paid aire, although that area of land is now being used for other purposes and *park4night.com* shows various free parking locations are being used instead. The town is also the home of the French motorhome parts company Narbonne Accessories (*www.narbonneaccessoires.fr*), which is a handy place for any habitation area bits and bobs you might need.

Carcassone consists of a large new town and a UNESCO-listed medieval fortress, it's the stone fortifications folks come in their droves to see.

Carcassonne

The setting for Kate Mosse's book *Sepulchre*, it has the fairy-tale mix of crenellated walls and rounded towers, inside which huddles a medieval town. The place has the feeling of a film set, with endless coaches of tour groups, tourist shops and restaurants, but it's an engaging and beautiful place to be. We stayed at Camping de la Cité, a 15-minute walk from the old town along a river (GPS: N43.200272, E2.353847).

To the south of Carcassone are other 'Cathar Castles', ruined hill-top fortresses which at one time sheltered members of a persecuted religious sect, the Cathars. Our guidebook told us the best of these was the Château de Peyrpertuse near **Duilhac-sous-Peyrepertuse**, which just happened to have a highly-rated free aire at the base of it (GPS: N42.861770, E2.565468).

The castle ruins stand impressively on a ridge, demanding a level of fitness to walk up to and around, and we huffed and puffed our way around, eyes-wide as we listened to an audio tour (recorded by an actor in English but with a comedically-strong French accent, like something from 'Allo 'Allo).

Château de Peyrpertuse, one of the best Cathar Castles

We've included **Trouillas** in this list as it's such a great example of the France Passion scheme (GPS: N42.61506, E2.81487). With a view of the snow-capped teeth of the Pyrenees, the Les Oliviers de la Canterrane olive farm (*www.lesoliviersdelacanterrane.com*) has an area set among the trees with large motorhome spaces available for free. The farm has also provided a service point, washing machines and even a communal area for travellers to sit and chat. We popped into the large shop and bought some top-quality oil and breads, thankful for such a relaxing place to stay after driving from Spain over the twisting N-260 and D914.

On another tour we'd driven over a higher part of the Pyrenees, using N-152 and N116, stopping near the historically-quirky 'Inland Spanish Island' of Llívia. We headed down the valley in the rain to the St Martin of Canigou abbey. Like the Basques to the West, Catalans live either side of the French-Spanish border, and we found ourselves a little perplexed to be in the Catalan village of **Casteil**, despite the fact we were in France. We stayed in the free parking (GPS: N42.5333, E2.39206), enjoying a walk up the switchbacks and the views from outside the abbey.

The Massif Central

France's best-known mountains are the Alps and the Pyrenees but, lying across a couple of French regions, the centre-south of the country also rises high into the sky, forming the Massif Central. The highest point is the Puy de Sancy at 1886m, *puy* being the French word for a small extinct volcanic cone.

The Massif Central was traditionally a relatively unvisited area of France, but the opening of the A75 motorway, known as *La Méridienne*, in 2010 has made access simple. We've used this motorway several times as a fast and free method of traversing France north-south. It's worth being aware that 30 miles of the A75 are over 1,000m above sea level, and can be snow-bound in winter, check the status of the road before your crossing (at *www.autoroutes.fr*).

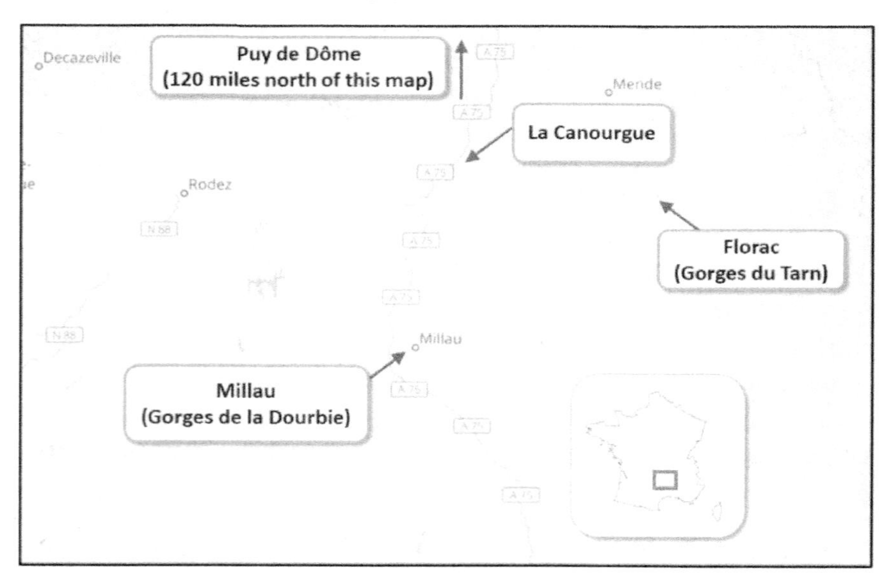

Starting in the far north, just west of Clermont-Ferrand, you'll find the 1465m-high **Puy de Dôme**, the highest volcano in the Chaîne des Puys mountain range. The views from the summit are worth the ascent, which you can walk up to or take a modern cog railway (we walked up and took the railway down, probably the wrong order!). Paragliders use the mountain to launch themselves into the sky, while behind you high on the peak lie the intriguing ruins of a Gallo-Roman temple.

Views of the Chaîne des Puys from the Puy de Dôme, Auvergne

During our visit the car parks below the volcano were all-but empty so we risked staying the night, although it was uncertain if it's allowed. For official places to stay, there are aires at Orcines (GPS: N45.788513, E3.010865) and Vulcania (GPS: N45.813229, E2.948484). There are several campsites in the area too, with Camping Domes (*les-domes.com*, GPS: N45.726331, E2.890024) being the closest. It's still a seven mile walk from the summit though, so a daytime stop-off in the car park might make sense, then head to the campsite after.

Most of our time in the Massif Central has been around 150 miles south of the Puy de Dôme. A famous sight in this area is the majestic white simplicity of the **Millau Viaduct**, which carries the A75 high in the air above the town of **Millau** to the east. The viaduct itself is a toll bridge, which we've always opted to avoid as we figure we get a better view of it, if we're not on it. Instead, we've taken the D991 and D992 through Millau, stopping in the town's aire on one occasion (GPS: N44.095933, E3.085827) and using the town to stock up on diesel, LPG and supermarket shopping on another. Running to the east of Millau along the D991, lie the **Gorges de la Dourbie**. As gorges go this is a pretty, gentle affair, easy to drive in a motorhome if you fancied a short detour from the A75.

The Millau Viaduct

If you're making a rapid crossing of the region the free aire at **La Canourgue** makes a good stop-off to break up the long journey (GPS: N44.433241, E3.211806). Only a couple of miles off the motorway, the town's quiet but pretty and has a couple of small supermarkets for any en-route supplies as you head north or south. The water's turned off in winter, so come with some in your tank.

Specifically built for tourists in 1905, the route through the **Gorges du Tarn** is worth a look. The official road runs down through Millau, but the real Route des Gorges starts north of Aguessac on the D907. The most impressive section is further along, north of Les Vignes on the D907BIS. There's a Camping Huttopia here (*europe.huttopia.com/site/gorges-du-tarn*, GPS: N44.2875389, E3.2328533). From this point, the gorge deepens, the white-rock sides close in and tunnels threaten to bar your passage (check your map before heading this way if you're over 3m high). We stayed the night at the free aire in **Florac** after driving the gorge (GPS: N44.325665, E3.590038).

France's Most Beautiful Villages

The French association *Les Plus Beaux Villages de France* (The Most Beautiful French villages) is well worth looking into. The website *www.les-plus-beaux-villages-de-france.org* lists out the villages which have made the criteria and publishes a yearly guidebook in English and

French. We've visited a few of the villages, they vary in character but were all worth a visit.

Gerberoy, one of France's 'Most Beautiful' villages, which has free motorhome parking nearby

All Our Overnight Locations Mapped Out

All the places above, and everywhere else we've stayed in France and across the UK, Europe and North Africa are mapped out here: *tinyurl.com/ourtourmap*. Each location has a link to the blog post we wrote while we were there, so you can easily see some photos and videos of that location, getting a feel for what it's like.

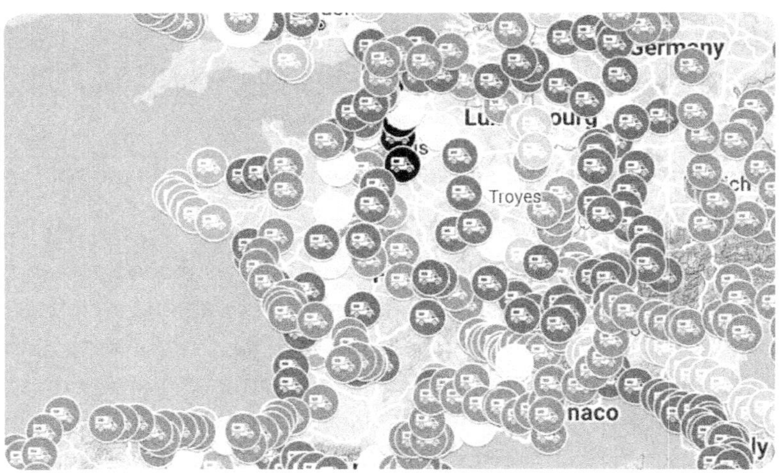

All our overnight locations are mapped out at *tinyurl.com/ourtourmap*

Our blog also has a selection of maps created by other motorhome bloggers, which you might find useful when planning your trips to France and beyond: *ourtour.co.uk/home/google-tour-maps-from-motorhome-bloggers*.

Route Planning

When you're pondering where to go in France it's worth being aware of some differences between the UK and French road networks. In this section we'll provide you with some knowledge to help you best lay out your travel plans before leaving home.

Types of Road in France

Crossing France on the slower, more scenic D roads

Formally, the French road network is divided into these types of roads:

- **Autoroutes** - the road number starts with an A, like the A16. Signs are blue and the road number (often displayed above the main blue sign) has a red background. These are motorways but are often only dual carriageway, and most are toll (you pay for these sections of road as you use them). On three-lane autoroutes motorhomes over 3,500kg can't use the left-most lane. Vans over 3,500kg also have to keep a minimum distance of 50m from the vehicle in front (this applies on all roads).

- **National Roads** - the road number starts with an N, like the N10 or with RN. Signs are green, and the road number has a red background. These are a mixture of dual and single carriageway, like UK A roads.
- **Departmental Roads** - the road number starts with a D, like the D31. Signs are white, and the road number has a yellow background. These are single carriageway roads, like UK B roads.
- **Municipal Roads** and **Forestry Roads**

Some roads also have an E number, shown in white against a green background. These are European routes, which cross international boundaries, and are made up of various roads. For example, the A16 in northern France is part of the E40, Europe's longest route, which crosses almost 5,000 miles to Kazakhstan.

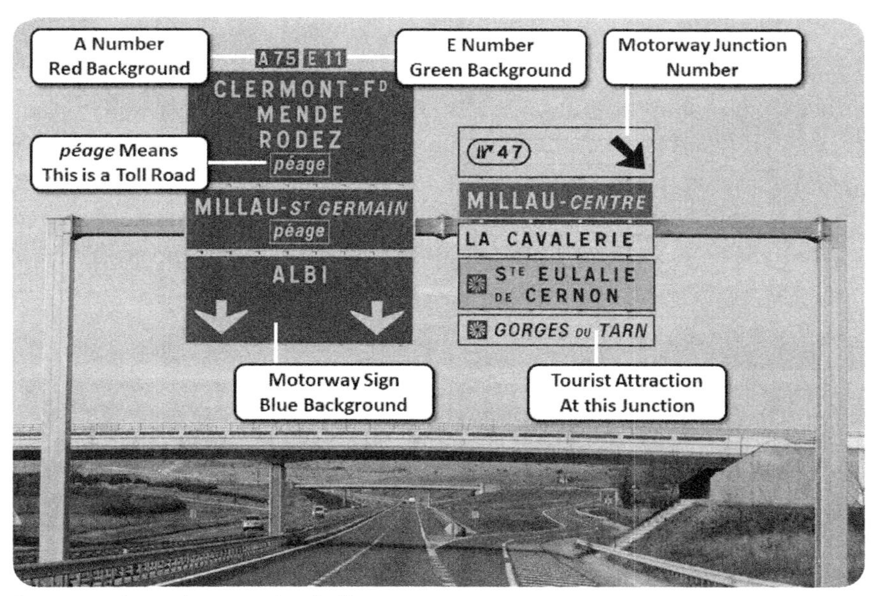

An example motorway sign in France

More informally, we look at the French road network like this:

- **Toll Motorways** - fast autoroutes which you pay to use, like the A28. We use these when we're in a hurry, but they're not cheap.
- **Toll-Free Motorways** - fast autoroutes which are free, like the A75. We use these to cross large sections of France for free.

- **Main Trunk Routes** - fast, sometimes dual-carriageway routes which are free of charge, like the N10. Again, these help cover larger distances in France and we plan out routes in advance to take advantage of them.
- **Yellow Roads** - the D roads are shown in yellow on our Michelin map. These are usually single carriageway but wide enough to pass oncoming vehicles. These smaller roads are comfortable to use but have low speed limits which are frequently reduced as they tend to cross through lots of towns and villages.
- **White Roads** - more minor roads are shown in white on our Michelin map. These can be single-width roads through miles of farmland with passing places. Our satnav happily uses them, but we tend to override it and avoid them if we have a choice.

Motorhome Speed Limits

Speed limits in France vary between road type, weather condition, vehicle type and whether you're in a town. Like the UK, France has an expansive collection of speed cameras, including mobile and average speed cameras. In addition, most French towns and villages have their own methods of speed management: chicanes, speed bumps, give-way signs granting priority to traffic coming from side roads and traffic light cameras which go red if they sense a speeding vehicle.

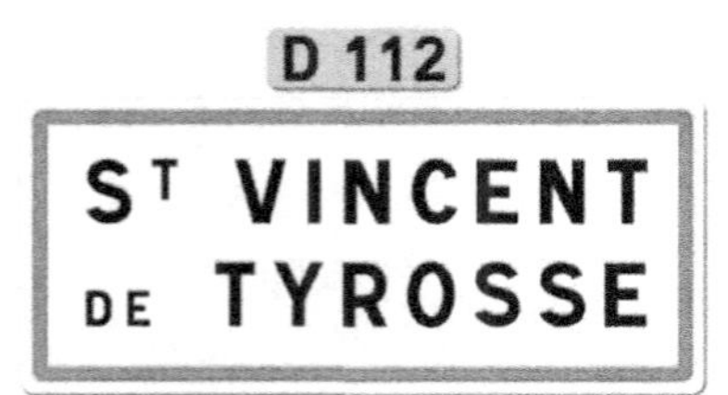

At a sign like this on the entrance to a town or village, the speed limit becomes 50kph unless another sign states otherwise (on faster roads it sometimes drops to 70kph).

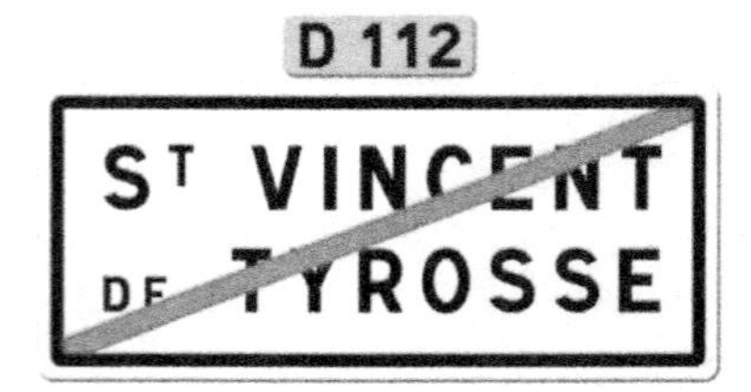

Leaving a French town, at a sign like this, the speed limit goes back up to what it was before.

For safety as well as legal reasons, it makes sense to be aware of the limits, the fact speed limits fall in poor weather and the fact there may be no '50kph' sign when you enter a town or village, just the name of the town (see above).

For a motorhome under 3.5 tonnes (also applies to motorhomes towing a trailer where the Gross Train Mass is less than 3.5 tonnes), these are the speed limits in France (mph figures are approximate).

- Toll autoroutes: 130kph (80mph) in dry weather, or 110kph (68mph) in adverse or wet weather.
- Dual carriageways and toll-free autoroutes: 110kph (68mph) in dry weather, or 100kph (62mph) in adverse or wet weather.
- Single carriageways with no central reservation separator: 80kph (50mph) or 90kph (56mph) in dry weather or 70kph (43mph) in adverse or wet weather.
- In towns: 50kph (31mph). Increasingly towns are applying 30kph (19mph) limits to parts of their centres, keep an eye out folks.

For a motorhome over 3.5 tonnes:

- Autoroutes: 110kph (68mph). Note that vans over 3,500kg can't use the left-most lane on a three-lane motorway. You must also leave at least a 50m gap from the vehicle in front of you.
- Dual carriageways: 100kph (62mph)
- Single carriageways: 80kph (50mph) or 90kph (56mph)
- In towns: 50kph (31mph), even if a sign indicates cars can drive at 70kph

For a motorhome towing a trailer, where the Gross Train Mass is over 3.5 tonnes (the GVW of the motorhome added to its towing limit):

- Autoroutes: 90kph (56mph)
- Dual carriageways: 90kph (56mph)
- Single carriageways: 80kph (50mph)
- In towns: 50kph (31mph)

In our 3.5 tonne motorhome we tend to drive at around 110kph (68mph) on autoroutes and fast, toll-free roads. Our satnav allows us to set a maximum speed, which it uses to calculate a more accurate journey time. This in turn avoids us seeing the arrival time creep upwards as we drive, which can be frustrating on long drives.

The 80kph or 90kph limits on single carriageways with no central divider can be very easy to accidentally exceed. Away from the main routes, most of the cross-country roads have this speed limit, despite being arrow-straight and (many of them) being nice and wide. The speed limit was lowered across France in 2018 from 90kph to try and reduce accidents, but parts of the country have moved the limit back up to 90kph on some routes. Look out for locally signed limits as you drive.

One of France's long, straight stretches of 80kph road

Some locals choose to ignore the limit, perhaps knowing exactly where all the speed cameras are, and will overtake at speed. You may sometimes find cars driving really close behind you before they pull out to overtake, this seems to be the way folks on the continent are taught. On occasion we find we're doing the limit but are still being tailed by a lorry, in which case we find the first opportunity to safely pull in and let the bigger vehicle past us.

Finally, when overtaking pedestrians and cyclists, you must leave at least a 1.5m gap (outside built-up areas) or 1m (in built-up areas).

To Toll or Not to Toll?

According to *google.com/maps*, the fastest route from Calais to Nice is around 1200km, or 750 miles, with almost all of it on toll motorways. The same route using only free roads is roughly the same distance, but the driving time goes from roughly 11 hours to 17 hours.

We wouldn't suggest any of these times are realistic (our motorhome wouldn't manage 130kph for long without drinking a serious amount of diesel), but you get the picture: trying to cross France without using the *péage* (toll) roads requires time and patience.

For toll costs, the amount you'll pay depends on which sections of toll road you use and your vehicle classification. The classes are given on the *autoroutes.fr* website. PTAC in French is equivalent to GVW in the UK, the Gross Vehicle Weight, shown on a sticker or plate attached to your motorhome. Our motorhome has a GVW of 3,500kg, is just under 3m high, has two axles and we don't tow a trailer, so we're class 2. Once you know which class you are, you can use the *www.autoroutes.fr* website to get an idea of the tolls you'll be charged. These are the various classes of vehicle for toll purposes:

Class 1 Light Vehicles 	• Overall height under 2m, GVW not exceeding 3.5 tonnes • If towing: overall height under 2m, GVW of tow vehicle not exceeding 3.5 tonnes
Class 2 Intermediate Vehicles 	• Overall height between 2m and 3m, GVW not exceeding 3.5 tonnes
Class 3 HGV or Bus with two axles 	• Overall height of 3m or more or GVW exceeding 3.5 tonnes

Class 4 HGV, Bus or other vehicle with three or more axles	•	More than two axles and height of 3m or more or GVW exceeding 3.5 tonnes
	•	Train with overall height of 3m or more
	•	Train with towing vehicle GVW over 3.5 tonnes

The height shouldn't include accessories such as solar panels or satellite dishes attached to the roof. Non-manned booths automatically calculate your height using a laser beam, so you may get placed into a higher class than you should be. Some folks hit the intercom button at the booth and tell them they're a *camping-car classe deux* (pronounced *camping car class der*), which sometimes works, sometimes not.

Our general approach with toll motorways is to avoid using them in order to save money, unless:

- We're in a hurry, perhaps to prolong the time we can spend in good weather in the south!
- We're travelling through an area of France we've seen many times, and are happy to bypass.
- We want to avoid areas where non-motorway traffic is heavy, like around Rouen or south of Biarritz heading into or from Spain.

Finding Fast, Toll-Free Routes

If you opt not to pay for the motorway tolls, there are still plenty of fast, toll-free roads in France which won't have you slowing down to 50kph as you go through towns and villages every five minutes. The *about-france.com* website is very useful for hands-on advice about driving in France, including detailed routes for crossing the country without either paying any tolls, or paying only minimal tolls.

This site also has an overview map showing all the main routes across the country, colour-coded so you can easily see which are free. We find this kind of high-level map very useful when planning long-distance routes. Here are some of the best toll-free routes we've used in the past:

- The free section of the A16 around the north France ferry ports.
- The free motorway network in Brittany.

- The N10 from Tours to Bordeaux.
- The A75 from Clermont-Ferrand to the Mediterranean coast (but you'll need to pay for the Millau viaduct unless you detour through Millau).
- If you're travelling from the ferry to the Alps, consider using the free motorways in Belgium and Luxembourg, then the free A31 into France.

When planning your trip, it's worth knowing that most lorries are banned from driving in France on a Sunday. This makes the day a great opportunity for doing long-distance drives, especially on non-toll motorway routes which they tend to use.

Low-Emission Zones (The CRIT'Air Scheme)

France has introduced a series of low-emission zones, restricting which vehicles can drive in certain areas within cities and wider areas to help manage the local air quality. The overall scheme is called *CRIT'Air* and applies to all vehicles, including those from abroad. Depending on where you plan to drive in France you might not necessarily need to do anything other than be aware of it.

The scheme has two types of low-emission zone:

- **Permanent Low-Emissions Zone** (now known as **ZFEs** - *Zone à Faibles Émissions*, previously known as ZCRs), including central Paris, Grenoble and Strasbourg. While these zones are permanent, the restrictions may only apply on certain days and at certain times.
- **Temporary Emergency Low-Emissions Zone** (known as **ZPA** - *Zone de la Protection de l'Air*, or a **ZPAd** if it applies to an entire department). ZPAs cover much wider areas than ZCRs. Restrictions are only enforced in these zones during periods of exceptionally poor air quality and are announced over the radio and in the local press. One easier way for non-French speakers to stay informed of the current ZPA status is the Green-Zones smartphone app.

To drive in any of these zones when restrictions are in place your motorhome needs an official sticker placed on the inside right of your windscreen, called a *vignette*. Without it (or with the wrong one) you risk an on-the-spot fine. There are six classifications of colour-coded vignette, the one you receive depends on the emissions of your vehicle. Each zone only allows vehicles with a minimum classification of vignette. You can buy the vignette from the UK through the official *www.certificat-air.gouv.fr/en* website for just a few pounds, so it makes sense to order one. You'll need to scan or photograph your V5C to send with the request.

The six classifications of CRIT'air vignette

The *www.crit-air.fr/en* website lists the cities covered by permanent ZFEs and areas with temporary ZPAs. The site also has an app called Green-Zones which shows all the European zones (zoom in to see the exact edge of each zone). This makes it easier to see if your journey will cross any of the areas affected.

Onward Touring

It's easy to travel from France to other European countries. Some of the most popular crossing points are shown below, and the bullet points offer a few tips for transitioning to the various surrounding countries.

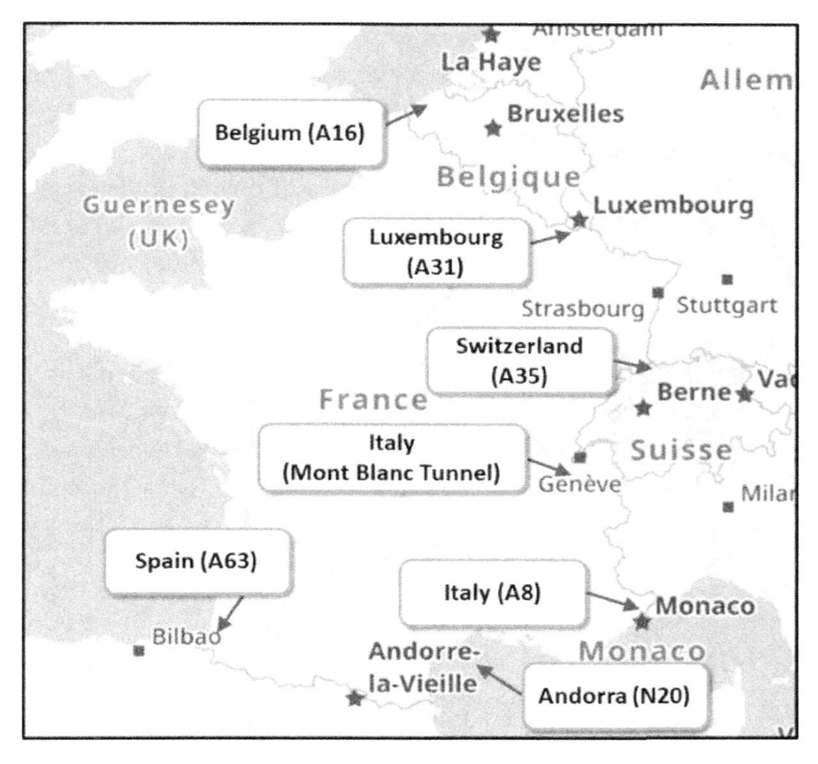

- **Belgium** - the motorways in Belgium are toll-free for motorhomes. They have a reputation for poor road surfaces, but we've found them to be generally good. The A16 across northern France into Belgium is free, as are the N225/A25/A27, which take you south-east towards Belgium around Tournai.
- **Germany** - the autobahn (German motorway) network is arguably the very best in Europe and is free to use.
- **Switzerland** - Switzerland isn't in the EU, so there are customs restrictions on what you can take into the country, such as a limited amount of meat. There are also customs borders, but often these are unmanned. We slow to a stop and peer into the booth to see if anyone is about before driving on. If your motorhome is 3,500kg or under, you'll need to buy a *vignette* (windscreen sticker) to use the Swiss motorways. If your van is over 3,500kg then you can pay online at *via.admin.ch/shop/config/psva*.
- **Italy** - the Alps stand between Italy and France, giving you three options for making the crossing: go over the mountain passes

(some are closed in winter and spring), go under using a tunnel (these can be expensive but are fast and open in winter), or head to the Mediterranean and use the A8 motorway and the E80 toll autostrada, which you can pay for in cash as you go.

- **Spain** - unless you fancy the adventure of driving up and over the Pyrenees, the easiest transition point is at Irun, at the west end of the mountain range. The hills are low here so there is no mountain pass to cross. The toll-free roads get busy, but you can use the A63 toll road to quickly get to Spain, then the AP-8 once over the border to avoid the slower routes. You can pay Spanish tolls in cash.
- **Andorra** - Andorra isn't in the EU, so there are customs restrictions between the two countries. As Andorra is also a tax-free zone there are often queues at the border for customs leaving the country. Diesel is much cheaper in Andorra, and there are fuel stations lined up ready to serve your needs once you're out of France. There are no toll roads in Andorra.

Rough Idea for Costs

Once you've bought, serviced and insured your motorhome, the biggest costs have already been covered. From that point the day-to-day cost of using the motorhome is low compared with other methods of travel. For a trip to France, these are the main costs you're likely to incur:

- The ferry or tunnel crossing. This cost varies with season, time of day (cheaper crossings are overnight) and time of year, vehicle size, how many passengers and whether you have pets. For two adults in a 6m long, 3m high motorhome we typically pay around £200 for a daytime return between Dover and Calais.
- If you're hiring a motorhome in France, expect costs of (very roughly) €100 to €150 a night. You'll also need to budget for flights or train tickets to and from the pick-up and drop-off locations.
- Overnight costs for campsites and aires can vary dramatically, from nothing by using aires and free camping to £50 a night or more for campsites, depending on how many people are in your party. Out of season, with an ACSI CampingCard you'll pay between €15 and €27 to camp for a night for two adults, a motorhome, a pet and electrical hook-up. In the summer prices at municipal campsites are

around €25 for the same party. Private campsites with swimming pools will be much more expensive. Paid aires tend to cost around €10 to €18 a night.

- Diesel and petrol costs were, very roughly, the same in France as in the UK at the time of writing. For an idea of current fuel prices across Europe see *www.tolls.eu/fuel-prices*.
- Bottles of wine and beer can be bought much more cheaply from supermarkets in France than in the UK. However, if you drink out at a restaurant or café, the prices are much more closely aligned.
- We find Food in French supermarkets to be slightly more expensive than in the UK.

Preparation for Your Trip to France

We'll now run through the preparations needed before heading off to France in more detail. There are quite a few points to cover, but please don't be put off. Once you've run through the process once it's much easier the next time!

We've listed out every possible scenario we can think of, many of which won't apply to you so you can ignore them. The *www.gov.uk/travel-abroad* site has a useful summary of the process of travelling abroad and returning the UK and is well worth a look.

Preparation for You and Your Passengers

These are the areas to consider for you and each of your passengers before leaving home for France:

- **Passports** - check their validity. They must be issued less than 10 years before the date you enter France. They must also be valid for at least 3 months after the date you plan to leave France. If issued before 1 October 2018, additional months may have been added to the expiry date, so your passport could be over 10 years old and still have over 3 months left. This passport would be rejected at border controls. Check carefully.
- **Driving Licenses** - check each driver's license remains valid for the whole trip and allows them to drive your motorhome's DVLA classification (if it's over 3,500kg they'll need class C1). If any drivers

are nearing age 70, they may need to renew their license. If you have a paper UK licence, check with the post office whether you need an International Driver's Permit (IDP).

- **Travel Insurance** - we suggest you buy travel insurance for yourself and each of your passengers to cover any healthcare costs. We tend to use one of the online comparison sites to find the level of cover we need at the best price. If you plan to ski, hike at altitude and so on, make sure your policy covers these activities.
- **EHICs and GHICs** - the European Health Insurance Card remained valid after Brexit, but they need replacing with a UK-issued Global Health Insurance Card (GHIC) once they expire. Both cards are provided free of charge. According to the NHS, the GHIC:

  "gives you the right to access state-provided healthcare during a temporary stay in the European Union (EU)".

  You can apply for GHICs from the NHS here: *www.nhs.uk/using-the-nhs/healthcare-abroad/apply-for-a-free-uk-global-health-insurance-card-ghic*.
- **Medication** - if any of your party needs prescription medication, make sure they have enough for the trip.
- **Euros** - while you can withdraw cash from ATMs in France using a UK-issued debit card, it may incur charges, so it's worth checking with your card issuer. We have a Nationwide current account which enables us to withdraw cash abroad without paying fees (*www.nationwide.co.uk*). Other cards are available without withdrawal fees abroad, like the pre-loaded CaxtonFX Card (*caxtonfx.com*). You may also want to obtain some Euros to tide you over until you're in a French town.
- **Internet & Phone** – check with your phone provider whether you can roam abroad, whether there is a per-day additional charge to roam, and what cap there is on how much mobile data you can use. If you need more mobile data, consider buying a SIM card abroad as described in *Staying in Touch in France* on page 147.
- **Ferry or Channel Tunnel Tickets** – After making your booking you won't be issued with tickets. Closer to the point of travel you'll receive a request to submit the name, date of birth and nationality of each passenger, known as 'advance passenger information' or

API. Once you've done this, you simply arrive at the Eurotunnel or ferry port check-in terminal and they'll process you electronically, no tickets required.

The Schengen Area and 90-in-180 Days Rule

France is part of the 'Schengen Area', which consists of 27 countries across Europe. When you enter the Schengen Area, such as crossing from the UK into France, you'll need to show your passport. Once you're inside the area you can travel from country to country without going through border controls. If, for example, you decided to nip from France into Germany, you might not even notice you'd crossed from one country into another.

Following Brexit, UK citizens can enter the Schengen Area without needing a visa. We can legally stay for up to 90 in a rolling 180 days. That could be all in one go, or several smaller trips. The day count doesn't get reset when you leave France, and the day you enter and leave France count as a full day. Also, the 90 days is for the entire group of 27 countries, so you can't legally stay for 90 days in France then go to Spain for 90 days, for example. Once your 90 days in France was done, you'd need to leave Schengen, by heading back to the UK or Ireland for example.

If you're making multiple visits into the EU (any holidays where you fly in count as well as your motorhome-based trips) it can be tricky to keep a track of how many days you've used. Websites like *ninety180.com* can be very helpful. On these websites you can input the days you've already spent in Schengen, and any planned future trips, and they will tell you whether you're within your 90-day limit.

Obtaining ETIAS Authorisation

As noted above, as long as we don't plan to work while abroad, UK tourists can travel visa-free to France and other Schengen countries for trips of up to 90 days in a rolling 180-day period. However, from 2025 (maybe, the date keeps going backwards) we'll need to apply for an 'ETIAS visa waiver' before travelling to France or any other EU country. This isn't a visa, and the process for obtaining it should be straightforward. The European Travel Information and Authorisation

System (ETIAS) will provide a new website where we will need to input details of travellers and get the go-ahead before travel.

There will be a small cost for each request (€7, about £6 per person), and authorisation will last for three years or until the passport expires. For more information have a look at *www.etias.info*.

Preparation for Your Motorhome

These are the areas to consider for your motorhome before leaving home for France (you can buy some of these at the ports, but expect to pay more if you do):

- **Insurance** - make sure your motorhome insurance covers travel to France. Most policies will cover at least short trips, but it makes sense to check with your insurer.
- **MOT and Road Fund License** - your motorhome needs to be legal in the UK while travelling in France, so your MOT and Tax need to be up-to-date throughout your trip.
- **Servicing** - we get our motorhome serviced once a year to try and reduce the risk of a breakdown when abroad.
- **V5C Log Book** - you need to carry the original of your motorhome's V5C. It's known as a *carte grise* (pronounced *kart greez*) and will need to be shown to police if asked or at a garage for repairs.
- **Light Deflectors** - you need to either use stickers on your headlights or (if your motorhome allows) to adjust the headlight beam manually so it doesn't dazzle oncoming drivers. This applies even if you don't plan to drive at night.
- **UK Sticker** – you'll need one of these attached to the rear of your motorhome unless your numberplate has a UK identifier (the old GB sticker or numberplate is no longer valid).
- **Angles Morts Stickers** – Since 1 January 2021, vehicles over 3,500kg driving in France require official 17cm by 25cm blind spot stickers placed in specified locations. You'll need one sticker on the rear on the French kerbside, between 0.9m and 1.5m from the ground, or as close as possible to this. A further sticker is needed on the sides, between 0m and 1m from the front of the van and again 0.9 to 1.5m from the ground (for more information, search *www.securite-routiere.gouv.fr* for 'angles morts').

- **Warning Triangle** - you'll need one of these to deploy in the event of an accident or breakdown.
- **Breathalyzers** – a French law was introduced requiring everyone carry two of these in their vehicle, but no penalty for not carrying them was ever introduced. This law was repealed in 2020, and we personally haven't bothered with these for years.
- **Reflective Jackets** - you need one of these for each occupant, stored within the motorhome so you can put them on before you step outside in the event of a breakdown.
- **Tyres** - you need to check these have enough tread to be legal (1.6mm in France) and they have no cracks or other damage. If you plan to travel to low-lying areas in winter conditions, you may want to consider fitting Mud and Snow (M+S) tyres. If you plan to head to mountainous areas between 1 Nov and 31 Mar, you'll legally need full winter tyres (Alpine-marked, 3PMSF tyres, a mountain symbol containing a snowflake) such as the Continental Vancontact Camper or the Michelin Crossclimate Camping. You'll also need to carry a pair of snow chains or socks. See *Mountain Driving* on page 118 for more details.
- **Gas** - you can't get Calor Gas bottles refilled in France so ensure you've either got enough gas for your trip, or fit Campingaz, or a refillable LPG system. This is discussed in detail later in this book.
- **Weight Check** - as in the UK, you can't legally drive in France if your motorhome is over its Gross Vehicle Weight (GVW). You may want to visit a weighbridge in the UK once your motorhome is fully loaded with passengers, fuel, water, food, pets and so on, to be sure you're not overloaded.

In addition to the above, you may want to consider the following items for your journey. None are mandatory.

- **First Aid Kit** - although there are pharmacies everywhere in France, we carry a basic first aid kit.
- **SatNav** or **Smartphone Navigation App** – make sure your satnav has maps for France. We use an OHREX Truck satnav with a full Europe map and lane assist. Our motorhome is 3,500kg, less than 3m high and 6m long and although this isn't a motorhome-specific satnav, it helps us choose routes which avoid weak or low bridges,

tunnels and narrow or steep roads. Note that it is illegal to use fixed speed camera alerts on your satnav in France; you have to disable this feature if you have it and you cannot use a mobile camera detector.

- **Breakdown Cover** - some insurers include European breakdown cover. If not, consider buying a policy from the AA, RAC, Green Flag, etc, checking it covers your age, weight and length of motorhome.
- **CRIT'Air Sticker** - as described previously, you may need one of these if you plan to drive into a French Low-Emission Zone. We've got one as they're cheap and easy to buy online.
- **Constat Amiable Form** - in the event of an accident in France you can optionally complete this form with the other party(ies) to send to your insurers. We once clipped wing mirrors with a van and had to complete one of these forms in French, which would have been easier if we'd taken an English-language version with us.
- **Roundabout Sticker** - you can buy transparent stickers which you place inside your windscreen to remind you which way to drive around roundabouts in France. We've never found we needed one as our motorhome is left-hand drive, and we get used to the roundabouts quickly.
- **Télépéage Transponder** - if you will use toll motorways frequently you may want to buy one of these and fit it to your windscreen (see *www.emovis-tag.co.uk* for more information). It will enable you to drive through dedicated lanes at toll booths, so you don't have to stop and pay there and then.
- **A Solar Generator or Portable Power Pack** – to keep your electricity costs down and flexibility up, you might consider taking a portable power pack or solar generator to France. These power packs are basically a leisure battery packaged in a plastic box designed to be carried around. They have a variety of connectors which you can charge your 12V equipment from. Many of them have a built-in inverter too, so they can run some of your 230V kit. You can recharge the power pack from the mains or from your van's aux power port (while driving to avoid depleting the starter battery). Some also allow you to plug in one or more portable solar panels to recharge the battery, hence the name 'solar generator'. Some well-known brands are Bluetti (*www.bluetti.co.uk*), Jackery

(*www.jackery.com*) and Goal Zero (*www.goalzero.com*). The power packs range in capacity from around 240Wh (roughly 20Ah of capacity) to over 2,000Wh (166Ah).

- **Spare Bulbs and Fuses** - we carry a set of spare headlight bulbs and all the different ratings of blade fuses our motorhome needs.
- **Spare Wheel** - there is no legal requirement to carry a spare wheel to France. Our motorhome came with one, so we carry it with a suitable jack and wheel brace.

Preparation for Your Pets

We took our pet dog Charlie, a Cavalier King Charles Spaniel, many times to France over the years. With the EU Pet Passport scheme, we found it easy to travel back and forth between the UK and France, although at first we were very nervous. The EU Pet Passport has been replaced with the Animal Health Certificate (AHC) since 1 January 2021 (unless you live in Northern Ireland), but the process for obtaining an AHC and using it to return to the UK is similar to the Pet Passport (although with important differences, see below).

This section runs through the preparation needed before you leave the UK and looks at some areas surrounding travelling around France with your pet.

Our dog Charlie heading for a play on a French beach

The Animal Health Certificate (AHC)

To take your pet dog, cat or ferret from Great Britain to France, you'll need an Animal Health Certificate (AHC) issued by your vet (unless you have a Pet Passport issued in Northern Ireland or in an EU country). Your pet will need to be at least 12 weeks old before you can start the rabies vaccination needed to obtain an AHC.

Each AHC covers up to five pets, but unlike the old Pet Passport scheme, you'll need a new AHC for each trip abroad. You'll need to get one from your vet in the 10 days before you will arrive in France, and the AHC will be valid for 4 months for travelling between EU countries before you return to the UK. You will need a new certificate for each trip you take abroad, even if you've still got a certificate from travel in the previous four months.

To obtain an AHC, your pet will need both:

- A microchip to be fitted.
- To be vaccinated against rabies (and boosted every 1 to 3 years, depending on the jab type and which country it's done in). You'll need to wait at least 21 days after the vaccination before your pet travels abroad, but there is no need for a subsequent blood test to prove the vaccination has worked.

Costs for an AHC will vary between vets, but we've seen quotes of between £110 and £180, depending on whether vaccination and microchipping has already been completed.

As well as obtaining an Animal Health Certificate, if your pet takes any medication, we found it best to obtain enough from our vets to cover the period of travel. We were also advised by vets in France to ensure our dog was covered for Leishmaniasis, which is most prevalent in the south of France. It's transmitted by sandflies and won't be stopped by your usual tick and flea treatment. We bought and used Scalibor Collars to protect our dog against Leishmaniasis.

If your pet is insured, check the cover applies abroad or consider buying a one-off holiday cover policy. Our dog wasn't insured, and we covered costs out-of-pocket, so we can't recommend any specific insurers.

Sourcing Pet Food in France

Be aware that EU law means you can't take pet food from the UK to France unless it's required for health-related reasons, and then you can only take 2kg of it:

europa.eu/youreurope/citizens/travel/carry/meat-dairy-animal

If you have a pet, you can search the websites for French supermarkets to see where their shops are, and to see which brands of dog food (*nourriture chien*) or cat food (*nourriture chat*) they carry:

- Carrefour - *www.carrefour.fr*
- Intermarché - *www.intermarche.com*
- Super U - *www.magasins-u.com*
- Auchan - *www.auchan.fr*
- Lidl - *www.lidl.fr*
- ALDI - *www.aldi.fr*

In practice this law doesn't appear to be enforced. We've never had our cupboards or fridge checked for human or pet food at the border and haven't heard of anyone else's who have. That said, the law exists and presumably spot-checks could be carried out at any time.

Booking a Pet Crossing to France

When booking a ferry or Channel Tunnel crossing, you'll need to declare your pets and pay for them. The Channel Tunnel charges £22 per pet, each way. You can travel with up to four dogs per vehicle, and you stay with your dog for the entire journey.

On most of the shorter ferry journeys your dog must stay in your motorhome on the ferry car deck. DFDS charge £18 per pet each way (*www.dfds.com*). P&O charge £15 per pet each way when they stay in your motorhome (*www.poferries.com*). On P&O's Dover to Calais route you can stay with your dog(s) throughout the crossing, by paying £12 per person for access to their on-board Pet Lounge. You can take your dog's bed and the lounge has complimentary hot and cold drinks, and access to an outdoor exercise area.

Brittany Ferries have different pet facilities depending on the ship. Some allow your pet to stay in your motorhome, others have kennels, and some have pet-friendly cabins (book early if you want one of these). They require dogs to wear muzzles when moving between your motorhome and kennel or cabin.

Crossing to France with Your Pet

When you arrive at the ferry port or Channel Tunnel terminal in the UK you'll be issued with a sticker or rear-view mirror hanger which shows the fact you have one or more pets with you. You just need to pop this in place and then board the ferry or train. At the Tunnel you'll need to park up and walk into a 24-hour Pet Reception building with your pet(s) to check them in.

Be aware that some breeds of dog which are considered 'attack dogs' under French law cannot be imported into France, and other breeds considered 'guard dogs' must have a pedigree certificate, be on a lead and muzzled in public and be insured against injury of third parties. Your vet should be able to advise whether your dog falls into either category or search the *www.service-public.fr* website for *chiens dangereux*.

Returning from France with Your Pet

When returning from France with your pet, you'll need to:

- Use an approved transport route and carrier. The France to UK ferry routes and the Channel Tunnel are generally approved routes. Search "pet travel: sea and rail routes and companies you can use" for a full UK government list.
- If you have a dog (this doesn't apply to cats or ferrets), you'll need a tapeworm treatment to be applied by a vet no less than 24 hours and no more than 120 hours (five days) before you arrive back in the UK. The vet will have to complete your pet's AHC when they do this. On trips less than five days, a UK vet can give the tapeworm treatment before you go to France.
- There's a map of vets who provide tapeworm treatments at this web address, although much of the info is from 2021 or before so adjust costs accordingly: *tinyurl.com/wormvetfrance*.

- When you check-in for your return journey your pet's micro-chip will be scanned and the AHC document checked.

All the vets in France we visited understood the Pet Passport scheme in detail and will understand the AHC system too. Worming treatment costs are around €25 to €50 per dog depending on the dog's weight and the vet. The vets generally require an appointment, which you can make before you leave the UK to give you peace of mind, or you can do it while abroad but allow plenty of time in case they're busy. Some vets will carry out a wider health check, and some will just provide the tapeworm treatment and complete the AHC.

We always returned to the UK with our dog via Dunkirk or Calais, and often used the *Clinique Vétérinaire du Haut Pont* vet in Saint Omer (GPS: N50.756190, E2.259662). The vets speak English and do a thorough check of your pets before issuing the worming treatment and completing the documentation. They're not the cheapest, but they do a good job. You need to call or use Facebook to make an appointment in advance.

Charlie at Clinique Vétérinaire du Haut Pont during his journey home

There is also a paid motorhome aire nearby on Rue de la Gaiete (GPS: N50.75643, E2.25952), although we've just parked on the roadside or in the town for free for the hour or so needed to complete the job.

Clinique Vétérinaire du Haut Pont
5 Rue de Belfort, 62500 Saint-Omer, France
Tel: 00 33 3 21 88 87 54
www.facebook.com/cliniqueveterinaireduhautpont62

Booking Your Crossing

When you've decided on your dates, you can book the ferry or tunnel crossing. This is straightforward, but here are a few things to consider.

Choosing Between the Tunnel and a Ferry

Here are a few thoughts for when you're choosing between using the Eurotunnel and a ferry:

- The English Channel isn't always as calm as it could be and if you suffer from sea sickness, it can be no fun worrying about and experiencing a rough crossing. In very rough seas crossings may also be cancelled. The tunnel doesn't have these problems.
- The Channel Tunnel is generally more expensive than ferry crossings.
- Tesco Clubcard vouchers can be used to reduce the cost of Channel Tunnel and Irish Ferry crossings or even get them for free.
- The tunnel takes 35 minutes, while the shortest ferries take at least 90 minutes, some many hours longer.
- You'll need to depart from Folkestone for the tunnel, but if you live in the west or south-west of the UK a ferry crossing to Brittany or Normandy may be more convenient.
- Ferries are more romantic in our eyes, at least when the sea is calm! The feeling as the white cliffs of Dover retreat into the distance is very different to that of being sat inside a train carriage which you can hardly detect moving.

Booking a Ferry

There are various ferry routes between the UK and France. Ferry costs for motorhomes vary depending on the dimensions of the vehicle -

usually the length and height, not the vehicle's weight. Costs also vary by sailing time. Typically, it's cheaper in the middle of the night, which will mean arriving in the dark which isn't ideal for a first time abroad.

You can either book direct on the ferry company's own website or use a broker site. By playing around with a few of these sites you'll get an idea how much your crossings are likely to cost.

- *www.aferry.co.uk* - brokers for ferry routes worldwide
- *www.directferries.co.uk* - brokers for ferry routes worldwide
- *www.ferrysavers.com* - brokers for UK-Europe ferry routes
- *www.dfdsseaways.co.uk* - direct with DFDS for UK-Europe routes
- *www.poferries.com* - direct with P&O for UK-Europe routes
- *www.irishferries.com* - direct with Irish Ferries for Dover to Calais
- *www.brittany-ferries.co.uk* - direct with Brittany Ferries for UK-France and Spain routes

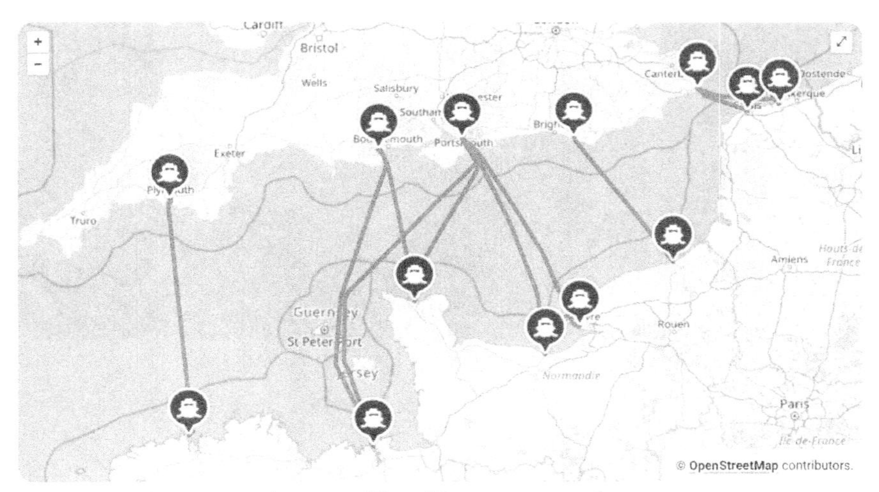

Ferry routes between UK and France, source: *ferrygogo.com*

Booking the Channel Tunnel (Eurotunnel Le Shuttle)

Eurotunnel tickets are booked direct through *www.eurotunnel.com*. Make sure you correctly state the height of your van, so you don't have to try (and fail) to squeeze it into a car carriage. Like with the ferry routes, Eurotunnel tickets are cheaper late at night or early in the morning and booking in advance can get you a cheaper deal. If you plan to go abroad regularly there is a frequent traveller scheme where you buy 10 crossings at a time. Eurotunnel accept Tesco Clubcard vouchers (*www.tesco.com/clubcard*), so by collecting these you could get your crossing for free.

You can use the Eurotunnel if you have self-refillable LPG tanks, or Calor-type gas bottles which are used for habitation only, but they must be turned off during the crossing. However, you can't use the Eurotunnel if your van's engine runs on LPG.

Our motorhome heading to France on the Channel Tunnel

Towing a Trailer

We've never towed a trailer (*remorque*) on our tours, but we've seen plenty of motorhomes which do. Carrying a second form of transport offers the opportunity to park your motorhome up somewhere for a while and use a moped, motorbike, car or quadbike to nip around the local area. We can see the attraction, although there are some areas to consider:

- You need to check the weight your motorhome can legally tow and check what restrictions your driving licence imposes.
- The additional weight and air drag will increase fuel consumption.

- A car, moped or motorbike will need its own insurance, tax and MOT as appropriate.
- The trailer and other transport must be secured against theft.
- A-frames are (probably, it's hard to pin down a definite source) illegal in France. To avoid potential trouble with the police we'd suggest avoiding using one to tow a car.
- Parking spaces in motorhome aires and most car parks are generally too small for a motorhome with a trailer, so you'll need to plan accordingly, checking photos of aires or using Google Maps to see if there is enough space to park with a trailer.

Enough space for a longer rig at this aire in France

Other Things to Consider Packing

In addition to your usual UK packing list, you may want to consider popping some of the following items into your lockers and cupboards:

- **A paper map.** Although we have a satnav and mapping applications on our phones, we still find our paper 1/200 000-scale Michelin Map of France to be very useful for getting an overview of an area, spotting low bridges, working out where toll booths are, etc.
- **An ACSI CampingCard** discount card and books for low-cost camping out of season.
- **A continental two-pin conversion lead adapter.** This will enable you to plug your mains hook-up cable into the old two-pin sockets still used on some French campsites and aires.
- **A hook-up reverse polarity tester plug, and conversion cable.** Some power supplies on the continent will have the live and neutral connections the wrong way around. This can potentially be

dangerous, leaving parts of appliances live even when they're switched off. To detect it you can buy a special plug which has lights showing when hook-up is detected, and whether it is reverse polarity. You can use a special cable adapter to correct the polarity.
- **Baked Beans and Teabags!** If you've any favourite British foods you can't be without, it's probably best to assume you can't get them in France and pack enough to keep you going. Be aware you can't legally take meat, dairy or animal products into the EU, although we've not yet heard of anyone's freezer being checked at Calais for cheese or bacon.

We've given a full sample packing list in the reference section towards the end of the book, which includes the above items and many more.

Renting a Motorhome in France

If you don't own a motorhome or campervan and want to rent one for a week or two, there are plenty of options to do this. The *mcrent.eu* and *www.francemotorhomehire.com* websites are an easy way to get a rough idea of how much different styles of motorhome will cost at different times of the year. Prices are (very roughly) around €1,000 (£900) a week.

When renting a motorhome, think about these points:

- Check pets are allowed if you have them.
- A motorhome may have more seats than it has three-point seatbelts. Check the rental van has enough properly belted seats, especially if you plan to use child seats in it.
- Even if a motorhome says it is four-berth, it may not comfortably sleep four people, or the bed arrangement may not work for your party. For example, a four berth may have two double beds, when a double and two bunk beds would work better for a couple with two older children.
- Motorhomes are relatively difficult to drive compared with cars. They're wider, so narrow roads take more concentration, and longer, so are harder to park. Our advice would be to rent the smallest motorhome or campervan which still allows comfortable sleeping and living, especially if you plan to move every day or two.

- Campervans may not have a loo or shower. If you plan to use aires or free camp, you'll need both.
- If you've not used a motorhome before, do a bit of research on how the water, fridge and electricity systems work. Be prepared for emptying a chemical toilet, it's not as bad as you might imagine but it's an, erm, interesting experience at first.
- When you pick up the van, get them to run through all these systems. Consider recording this on your phone so you can check it afterwards:
    - Turning water heating on and off
    - Turning space (air) heating on and off
    - Turning the gas supply on and off
    - How to use the fridge (not as obvious as you might think)
    - Where the diesel or petrol filler cap is and how to open it
    - How to check how full the fresh and grey water tanks are
    - How to check how much charge is left in the leisure battery
    - How to empty the grey water
    - How to empty the toilet and refill with chemicals
    - How to refill the fresh water tank
    - How to hook-up the van to the mains electricity
    - How to get the van level on ramps
    - How to use the TV and satellite, if there is one
    - How to assemble the bed
    - How to start and move the van (handbrake, gearbox, reversing camera)
- A general piece of advice: if there are two adults get one to spot for the driver when reversing. It's easy to reverse into a low wall or high tree even with a reversing camera. Developing good hand signals removes the need for frantic shouting and banging on the side of the van.
- If the motorhome is over 3500kg GVW (total permissible weight), you'll need a class C1 entitlement on all drivers' licences. Most rental vans will be under 3500kg GVW.
- Check what's provided in the van. Cooking utensils, pots and pans will probably be there, but maybe not bedding or toilet chemicals.
- Ask what level of insurance is provided, and whether breakdown cover is included.

- If you can, read independent reviews of the company so you get an idea how they treat their customers, what conditions the vans are in, whether they speak English and so on.

Day-to-Day Motorhome Life in France

This part of the book assumes you've done your preparation and are ready to depart for France! The following sections look at getting to France, travelling around, finding great places to stay, buying fuel, eating out, staying in touch with home and generally making sure you enjoy yourself!

Travelling to and Using the Ferry and Tunnel

The day has finally arrived, and you're heading off to the continent! Here are a few lessons we've learned from our time travelling to foreign parts.

Check the Foreign Office and Traffic England Websites

We've found ourselves sat in long queues and have nearly missed our crossing as a result. We now check the government website *www.gov.uk/foreign-travel-advice* before we leave, for information on any potential disruption such as strikes or protests. We also check *trafficengland.com* or *www.google.co.uk/maps* (using the Traffic layer) to see if there's any major disruption on the roads to our destination.

EU Duty Free Allowances

Each passenger over 18 can take the following from the UK to France, regardless of whether you paid duty, or bought the goods duty-free (on the ferry for example):

Goods	Allowance Per Passenger
Wine	4 litres of still wine
Spirits	1 litre of spirits or alcohol over 22% ABV OR 2 litres of sparkling wine or fortified wine or other alcoholic drink less than 22% ABV
Tobacco	200 cigarettes OR 100 cigarillos OR 50 cigars OR 250g tobacco OR any proportional combination of the above
Other Goods	€430 (€150 if under 15) worth of any goods such as fragrances, cosmetics, souvenirs, gifts and electrical products

EU Import Restrictions on Meat, Dairy and Plants

Following the UK's departure from the EU, we're unable to take meat, plants, plant products or dairy products from the UK to France. This includes most fruit and vegetables and pet food. Very limited quantities of certain types can be imported for health reasons. See the following sites for more details:

food.ec.europa.eu/animals/animal-products-movements/personal-imports_en

www.gov.uk/visit-eu-switzerland-norway-iceland-liechtenstein

Anecdotally these restrictions aren't enforced, but they could be at any time, especially if there's an outbreak of disease or change in the political situation. As we're never had our fridge or cupboards checked for food crossing into France, and haven't heard of anyone else who has, we're not sure what the implications of being caught with tins of pet food or sausages and bacon in the freezer will be. The law is clear though and obviously we can't advise anyone to ignore it. If you choose to do so, it's entirely at your risk folks.

The Dartford Crossing

If you use the Dartford Crossing on the eastern M25 motorway between 6am and 10pm, make sure you pay the toll charge the day before or by midnight the day after (*www.gov.uk/pay-dartford-crossing-charge*). If you forget, you'll be fined. We used to pay for two trips at the same time, so our return journey was covered too. We then wrote it in the diary, so we didn't forget we'd already paid.

We set up an account which automatically deducted the charge from our bank when we used the crossing. However, after not making the crossing for a couple of years we found our account had been suspended. Luckily, we realised and made the payment manually.

Overnight Stays Before Leaving the UK

We live in the East Midlands, so tend to travel most of the way to the ports the day before and then get the ferry/Eurotunnel the following morning. For those travelling from further afield, a well-placed campsite, aire or Brit Stop (*www.britstops.com*) can be handy to bed down for the night.

The motorhome aire at Canterbury (GPS: N51.26232, E1.10247, post code: CT1 3EJ) is a good stopover option about 25 minutes' drive from Dover and Folkestone. The aire, which is at New Dover Road Park and Ride, has a service point, so you can fill up and empty your loo and water tanks. The price includes a bus to Canterbury and back. It costs only a few pounds (see *www.canterbury.gov.uk*), which you pay when you're about to leave, however you'll need to pay for two days at the pay machine, as the payment for each day lasts until midnight.

Getting On and Off the Ferry

To get to the port, we use the 'car ferry' points of interest in our satnav, although they're also well sign-posted on all the main routes. Your ferry company should tell you when you need to arrive, usually 30 to 45 minutes before the sailing, but up to 2 hours at busy times. We always end up being early and if there's an earlier ferry with space we've been placed on it, otherwise we get directed where to wait. On one occasion we were several hours early so we were redirected out of the port and had to find somewhere on the roads outside to wait.

Once we're at the port, we never fail to get a little nervous. Ferry ports always seem to be a maze of lanes and signs, although they invariably manage to funnel us to the right place. It helps to have a passenger on 'sign lookout' duty, and it's a good idea to check your ferry company's website for details about the process at the port you are leaving from.

The first set of booths you'll reach are for French Border Control. Hand over your passports to be checked and stamped. Make sure they've stamped them all, and with the correct date. This will be used when you leave France (or any Schengen Area country) to check you haven't exceeded the 90-in-180 days rule. This system is due to be replaced with an electronic one in 2024 or 2025 (with a system called the EES), but for the time being these passport stamps are used.

Schengen passport stamps – entering France (left) & leaving (right)

You may get a 'spot check' at UK Border Control, we've had this a couple of times. We were asked to drive into a large hanger where two officers checked under the motorhome while another one got inside for a look around. They asked us a few questions, including a slightly comical one about whether we had any knives on board (we have a kitchen!), and we were on our way in just a few minutes.

After UK Border Control, you'll be routed to the ferry company's booth where you need to hand over passports for everyone in your vehicle, including pets. They'll hand back a boarding card which hangs from your rear-view mirror and tell you a lane number to head for. If you have a dog with you, it's worth asking where the designated dog walking area is located, so they can stretch their legs before the crossing.

Once the barrier is lifted you drive into the port and follow the signs to your lane. There can be hundreds of lanes but if you forget which one is yours it should be written on your boarding pass. Once you've found your lane, drive down it and queue up behind anyone already in it. If you're first, stop at the end of the lane, turn your engine off and wait. At this point we tend to flip the fridge back onto gas, walk the dog, stick on headlight deflectors, make some snacks and drinks to take on board, and start to get excited.

At some point the ferry staff will indicate you can start boarding, or you'll notice the vehicles in your lane (or the one next to you) start moving. We turn the gas off at this point if we haven't already, turn the fridge onto 12V (so it's ready when we leave the ferry) and transfer frozen cool blocks from the freezer into the fridge in warm weather. We then follow the port staff's guidance onto the ferry. There is often a ramp up onto the ferry, take it slowly, especially if you have a long or low overhang at the rear of your motorhome. It can also be worth hanging back a little if you are in a queue, so you don't have to stop and start on the ramp.

Once on board, members of the ferry staff will direct you into a lane and ask you to drive close to the vehicle parked in front of you. Keep going until they tell you to stop, which is usually just that bit closer than you think you can get. Turn off your engine, leave the van in gear and pull the handbrake on. It's not really worth turning your alarm on, as all the car alarms go off when the ferry starts moving (you can sometimes see some of the car deck from inside the ferry).

At this point we would open the skylights for our dog, close the blinds or curtains, make sure he had plenty of water, and grab our snacks before heading upstairs. Remember the deck number you're parked on and, on some ferries, the colour of the stairwell, so you can find your van again!

During the crossing we turn off our phones as the charges for using the ferry's mobile network for calls and data are often very high. It's also worth changing your satnav to kilometres and the time on your watches and smartphones, as France is one hour ahead of the UK.

When you arrive at your destination, an announcement will be made in several languages, including English, to let you know when to head to the car deck. This often seems to be made after the ship has docked. Follow everyone else down the stairs and return to your van. Start up your satnav and wait for the ferry doors to open. Staff will indicate when it's your time to drive out.

There's no need to start your engine until the vehicle in front of you is moving, as you may be waiting a while for the lanes around you to clear first.

Leaving the port of Calais

There are no checks when you get off the ferry, so you'll be driving straight out of the port and onto the local road network. Having your satnav on and programmed helps it quickly plan a route once you're out of the ferry. Follow everyone out into the port (or the road signs if you are at the front), remembering to keep in the right-hand lane if there is one, to let faster folks overtake. Then just follow your satnav or look for signs to the road you need. The fear of messing this part up is always there for us, but trust us, it's easy. Before you know it, you'll be cruising along, although most likely still concentrating hard!

Using the Channel Tunnel (Eurotunnel LeShuttle)

Getting to the Channel Tunnel is simple: drive down the M20 southbound and follow the signs for passenger traffic (not freight). LeShuttle advise you search your SatNav for "UK Check-in booth" and not to use the postcode CT18 8XX. Alternatively, the GPS co-ordinates are: N51.093389, E1.119278 and the What3Words address is //certainty.standards.willpower.

Aim to arrive between 45 minutes and two hours before your train is due to leave. Have the debit or credit card you booked with to hand, plus your reservation number. You'll be stopped by a barrier next to a machine. If you booked online your registration plate will be read by the check-in machine, otherwise, check yourself in using the machine.

Eurotunnel allows you to take an earlier train if there is space available. The machine will show you the train times and any additional charge if applicable. Select the train you want, and the machine will print out a boarding pass for you to hang from your rear-view mirror. You can now drive to the waiting area, where you'll find toilets, shops, the Pet Reception building and a dog walking area, or head through British and French passport and customs controls. Make sure French immigration stamps each passport with your entry date. You'll need this when you leave France (or any other Schengen Area country) to prove you've not stayed more than 90 in a rolling 180 days.

After these booths you may be directed to one side to ensure that your gas bottles are switched off, so make sure they are before you go through the final barriers and queue for your train. As you won't have access to gas on the train, it's a good idea to boil some water and pop it in a flask to make drinks on your journey before you reach these barriers.

Once the barriers raise, about 25 minutes before departure, follow the directions and head onto the train. Take your time at the entrance to line yourself up. Drive forwards through the carriages, leaving a gap so you don't end up reversing if the carriage in front is full. Park so you're up close to the vehicle in front of you (a member of staff will help), turn your engine off, leave the van in gear and pull the handbrake on. The staff also suggest you leave a window partly open to help with any changes in air pressure.

Some folks have mentioned to us that the carriages on the Chunnel are too small and claustrophobic. We've only used the Chunnel a couple of times but found there was easily enough room to drive a 2.2m wide motorhome into the carriage, get out and walk up and down. It was also great to be able to stay in our motorhome with our pooch. The crossing seemed to take about 8 minutes, OK, it was 35 minutes, about a third the time of a Dover to Calais ferry. Sadly, you can't see the water during the crossing, but there are small windows so you can see when you're not in the tunnel.

During your crossing you might want to change your satnav to show kilometres and move the time forwards an hour. Our watches and smartphones automatically switch to French time.

There are no checks when you get off the train, so you'll be driving straight out of the station and onto the local road network. Have your satnav on and programmed, so it gets a signal quickly once you're off the train. Follow everyone out into the station, or the signs if you are at the front, remembering to keep in the right-hand lane if there is one, to let faster folks overtake. Then just follow your satnav or look for signs to the road you need.

Driving in France

Once your wheels touch down on French tarmac, the following sections should help you get safely to your first destination and beyond.

Driving on the Right

We (the UK) drive on the opposite side of the road to France, and indeed everyone else in Europe apart from Ireland, the Channel Islands and the Isle of Man. The thought of driving on the right has frankly terrified us in the past, but the experience itself has always been more exhilarating than fearsome. Being sat in the van waiting to get off the ferry, we always have to remind ourselves which side of the road we need to drive on and set up satnav to nag us about it too.

We found roundabouts are surprisingly easy to navigate on the right, as there is usually plenty of signage and other traffic to follow. We got the hang of them almost straight away.

The hardest part for us is at 'change points', such as a single carriageway road becoming a dual carriageway, where we might forget whether the left or right lane is the slow one. Or when we turn out of a one-way street or car park into two-way traffic, we have found ourselves on the left for a moment. This rarely happens on day one, when we're concentrating hard on getting it right, but after a few days when we're more confident and less alert. We've never had an accident in this way, perhaps as we only get the lane wrong when there's no other traffic.

We use a couple of pieces of tape stuck to the bottom of our windscreen to help the judge where we are on the road. When the driver looks at the left piece of tape, it lines up with the left side of the road, that's as far across as we can go. Ditto for the right piece of tape.

We've used both left and right-hand-drive vehicles to drive in France and both are fine. Our preference is for a left-hand-drive motorhome though, simply because it gives the driver the best view down the road when overtaking or passing parking vehicles. With someone sat in the passenger seat who can look up the road for the driver, right-hand-drive vans are no problem.

Traffic Lights in France

The first time we sat in our motorhome staring at a flashing yellow light was an interesting one. What do we do? There was no-one else around, so we cautiously drove through it, wondering what on Earth was going on. It turned out that was exactly what we were supposed to do! These flashing orange lights aren't traffic lights; they're there to tell you to proceed with caution (and sometimes to give way to the right).

Conversely, there is no amber light displayed after red at traffic lights, they just go green, boom, go, go, go! The amber light is shown after green though to warn you to stop (so they go: red-green-amber-red).

Roundabouts

Almost all French roundabouts work pretty much the same as in the UK, except for the fact you drive around them anti-clockwise of course. You have to give way to vehicles already on the roundabout, so those to your left in France. Lorries and some other vehicles will use the right-hand lane to turn left. In other words, be wary of vehicles going all the way around the roundabout in the outside lane.

Using French Toll Roads

French toll roads are a great way to cross large parts of France quickly and safely. They tend to be dual carriageways, not three or four lane motorways like you might expect but nevertheless are frequently devoid of traffic. You can work out which roads are toll (paid) by checking your paper map or looking for the word *péage* on road signs. If we want to avoid paying for tolls, we set up our satnav to avoid toll routes, which works well.

A *péage* sign, indicating you're approaching toll booths in 400m

A set of toll booths in France

You can pay for your French tolls in two ways:

1. using cash/card at a payment booth (some are manned, many are just a machine),
2. or you can use *télépéage*, which means using an electronic tag in your motorhome to track which sections of road you've used and make payment electronically.

Using cash or card at toll booths is a simple process:

- When you join a toll road, you usually have to stop at a machine and take a ticket. This isn't always the case though, some are sort of ‘pay as you go’, so you stop at the barrier and pay for the stretch of road you have just used.

- When you leave the toll road you will again reach a set of toll booths. If you have a ticket you pop it in the machine. The amount owed in Euros is shown on a screen, and you make payment using either cash or a credit or debit card. UK cards work, and you can often just tap them on the machine.

Paying at a toll booth (*Espèces* means cash)

A few notes on this process from our own experience:

- Lanes to the left at the toll booths sometimes have a height barrier which will be too low for a motorhome. They’re easy to spot as you approach.
- Lanes with an illuminated green arrow accept credit cards and cash. Lanes with a card symbol accept only credit cards. Most booths are unmanned these days. If you’re using a card, you can simply hold it against a sensor and payment will be taken without typing in your PIN number.
- The toll booth lanes aren’t wide! We really slow down when entering them to avoid hitting the sides.
- While the machines usually have two sets of slots to put your ticket in and pay, we find the car one too low and the lorry one too high so the driver may have to lean out the window a bit to insert the ticket, cash or card into the toll booth machine.

- Most motorhomes will be Class 2 but may be incorrectly charged the higher Class 3 rate if a satellite dish pushes the height over 3m. There is an intercom button on the machines which some motorhome travellers have reported using to tell them they are *classe deux, un camping car*.

The alternative to cash or card payment is to get a *télépéage* transponder. You fit this to your windscreen, and then use the lanes marked with an orange *t* (avoid those to the left with a height barrier). You don't need to lower your window, take a ticket or make cash or card payment. Instead, you drive slowly towards the barrier, it reads your transponder, beeps and shows a green light then automatically raises. To use this system, you need to source your transponder from one of several issuers, such as *www.bipandgo.com* or *www.emovis-tag.co.uk*. You'll typically be charged for the transponder, plus a monthly fee and the cost of the tolls.

You can check the conditions on motorways before you set off using the *autoroutes.fr* website:

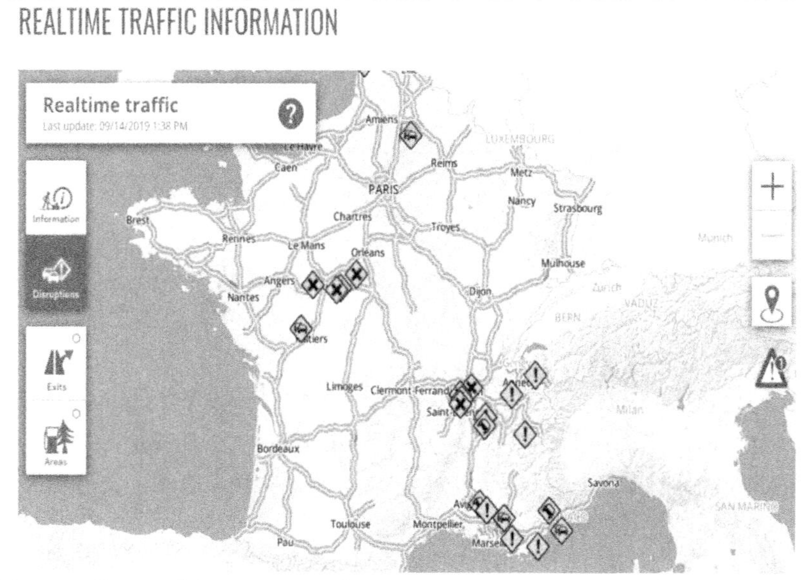

Realtime traffic conditions on French motorways on *autoroutes.fr*

Giving Way to the Right

France has an interesting old traffic rule called *la priorité à droite*. Under this rule, you must (under certain conditions) give way to traffic coming from sideroads on the right, even if you're on the 'main road'. The rule applies when you arrive at a crossroads or sideroad which has no painted 'stop' or 'give way' marking or traffic lights.

You'll spot the following *la priorité à droite* signs as you drive in France.

A red triangle containing two crossed lines: you must give way to the right at this junction.

A red triangle with a thicker arrow pointing ahead: you have priority at this junction.

A yellow diamond with a white surround: the priority to the right rule no longer applies.

A yellow diamond with a white surround, and a black bar through it: the priority to the right rule now applies.

Don't worry too much about *la priorité à droite* rule. We find it impossible to keep track of the yellow diamonds so never know if we're in an area where the rule applies or not. We find the rule tends to be used mostly in smaller towns and villages, and larger ones have 'give way' signs and paint on side roads. When we're in these towns we keep an eye out for the crossed-lines sign and look at the ground on side streets to see if there is a stop or give-way line painted on it.

In several years of driving in France we've gotten this rule wrong only two or three times (that we know of), which has resulted in nothing more damaging than a car horn being blown.

Finally, *la priorité à droite* applies in car parks! Again, unless there are road markings showing who has priority, then cars coming from the right can (and will) pull out on you, as they have the right to do so. This has caught us out before, but again no damage was done.

Bad Weather

Not wanting to state the obvious: if the weather when driving is very bad, slow down. Legally the speed limit drops on motorways, but even then, if you can't see very well because it's raining or hailing so hard, put your lights on, put your hazards on if necessary and if it's safe to do so, consider pulling over if things get really hairy. We've only had to do this twice in several years of motorhome travels (never on a motorway), but we're glad we did one of the times as the storm felled several trees along our route.

A sign indicating the speed limit drops when it's raining

Crawler Lanes

You may come across crawler lanes on the right side of long inclined sections of multiple-carriageway roads. These are marked out with a VEHICLES LENTS sign and have longer white dashes than the other lanes. If you're unable to keep up with the other traffic, pull into this lane (we always do). A FIN DE VOIE VEHICULES LENTS sign indicates when the lane is about to merge back in with the other lanes.

Mountain Driving

France has some wonderful mountains for you to explore in your motorhome. Given the difficulty in building roads in such challenging environments, they're rarely dual-carriageways and you will encounter some conditions which you might not be used to. This section gives some advice from personal experience on handling these types of road.

Serpentine bends as we ascend to Plaine-Joux, north of Mont Blanc

All our advice comes with an overall caveat: these roads often look far worse than they really are when you're driving them. We can recall staring up with nerves at the Col du Galibier (and lots of other mountain passes) but driving over it the following day with huge smiles and zero issues.

Traffic on the more sinuous routes tends to be light or mainly tourists, so you don't have the stress of being 'pushed' by lorries and commercial vans, so you can take your time.

Dealing with a narrow road on the D925, the Cormet de Roselend

The D roads in the mountains are sometimes too narrow for two vehicles to pass at any speed. It really helps to have a good sense of how wide your motorhome is, and to not be in a hurry. As mentioned, we use a couple of pieces of tape stuck to the inside bottom of our windscreen to help judge where we are on the road. If it gets tight we swap from using these to the wing mirrors, or in extreme cases the passenger is deployed as a spotter and uses hand signals to guide the driver through as seen in the photo above.

Keep an eye out on your map and for road signs letting you know if there is a tunnel ahead, and make sure there are none too low for your motorhome - we have our height, width and length written down and on display in the cab. We're just under 3m high, and we're rarely too tall for these tunnels. You need to turn your lights (*feux*) on before entering a tunnel and can turn them off again when you're out the other side. If you use the big Alpine tunnels to cross to Italy (the Mont Blanc or Fréjus tunnels), then you'll need to pay a toll each way and comply with safety regulations, specifically speed limits and maintaining a specified distance from the vehicle in front of you.

If you opt to drive over any of the *cols* (mountain passes), then check they're open first. Even in June some passes are closed due to snow and ice falls onto the road. *alpenpaesse.de* is a good resource to check whether French mountain passes are open. The passes often have somewhere to park at the top to admire the view or even stay overnight (with wonderful starlit night skies). Check *park4night.com* or a similar resource for overnight parking information. Also check the weather: it can be exposed in these high places, some of them over 2,000m, and being blasted by the wind all night isn't relaxing.

Mountain passes will also test your brakes. Some of the descents can go on for 10 miles or more. We get our brakes and brake fluid inspected yearly, making sure the garage knows we're heading into the high mountains, so they need to be in perfect condition. Even so, if we try and use our brakes all the way down, we risk overheating them (known as 'cooking the brakes'). We've only done this a couple of times, and the spongy feeling of the brake pedal was frightening, as pressing down didn't result in the van slowing down! We now make heavy use of engine braking, where we keep the van in a low gear on descents, only using the brakes from time to time, and pull over on very long descents where safe, to check the wheels aren't too hot. As a basic rule, if we use 2nd gear to drive up a hill, we use 2nd (or even 1st) gear to drive down it.

Mountains also present the possibility of snow and ice from autumn to spring. If you plan to drive in the mountains between 1 November and 31 March, you need to fit 3PMSF-marked (full winter) tyres (until 1 Nov 2024 M+S tyres will be allowed). You'll also need to buy and carry a set of snow chains or socks. This law applies to regions in the Alps, Corsica, the Massif Central, Jura, Pyrénées and the Vosges, shown on the map below. Check *tinyurl.com/francewinter* (in French) for more information on this law.

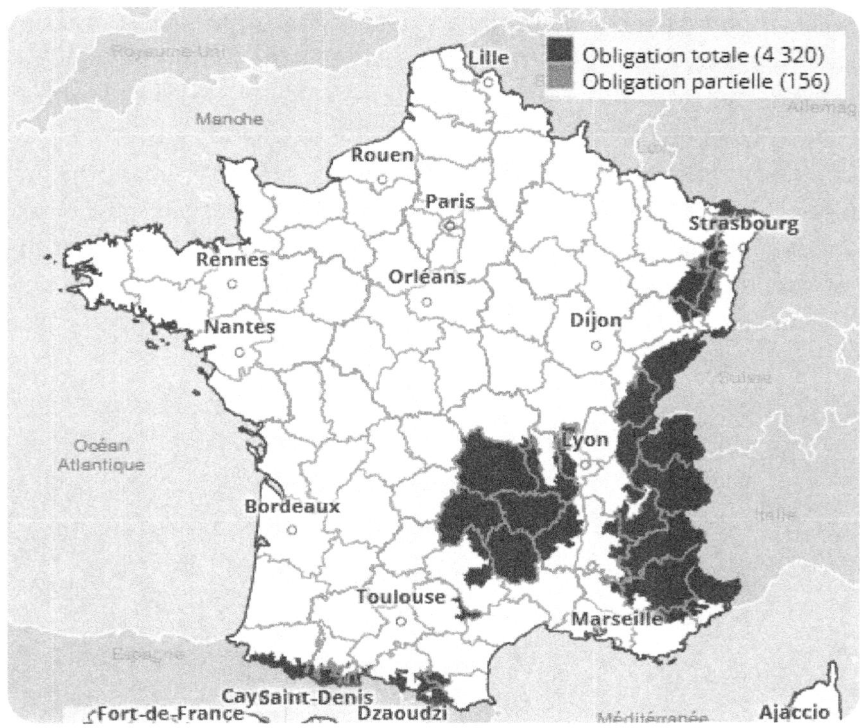

Regions of France covered by the mandatory winter tyre/chain law

When you're out on the road, the following signs indicate when you're in a region where the winter tyre/chain rule applies (the left sign, which has a red surround) or no longer applies (the right sign, all in black).

Signs at the entrance & exit of a mandatory winter tyre/chain zone

Practice putting snow chains or socks on, seriously, it's worth making sure you know how they fit. Put them on your motorhome's drive wheels, the front pair for us. Our snow chains are incredibly fiddly, especially if your hands are freezing or you're wearing gloves and you don't want to be outside your van for ages trying to fit them for the first time when it's snowing. Chains are only needed on packed snow or ice, and we've only ever used ours once as we don't tend to drive in the mountains in winter, but we have fitted them several times to practice. Special parking areas for fitting chains are sometimes provided called *aires de chainage*.

Even outside winter, you must fit chains or socks if you pass this round sign when the road is covered in snow. The rectangular sign underneath advises winter tyres (without chains) are acceptable in this case.

Finding Great Places to Stay

France is awash with great places to stay in your motorhome. Finding them isn't difficult once you know which websites, apps and databases everyone uses. This section runs through some of the best resources we've come across.

To Book or Not to Book?

First up let's look at the question of whether you need to book your overnight stays or not. When we first headed to France, we made sure we booked our first night or two's campsite stays. This reduced our stress levels as we knew we'd have somewhere to wind down after the journey, but even on those initial forays we didn't book every night. These days we hardly every book ahead.

If you use the aires network, then you can't book anyway (except for Camping-Car Park aires, see page 129). If you use campsites, they're not often full, and outside of peak season (July and August) there's usually a good choice of pitches. If you do want to stay in a specific site in summer or want to have the assurance of knowing exactly where you'll stay each night on your trip, then of course you can book most campsites ahead of time.

If you don't want to phone the site, several websites let you book online, including *www.allcamps.co.uk*, *www.sandaya.co.uk* (for 4- and 5-star sites) and *www.pitchup.com*.

French Campsites

French campsites are mostly good (or great) quality, even the cheap-and-cheerful municipal sites which are managed by the local mayor. With roughly 10,000 campsites on offer, you could stay in a different one each night for over 20 years and you'll still not have seen them all.

Camping at Muides-Sur-Loire

Here are some tips for finding and using great French campsites:

- French campsites are formally classified using a star rating, from one to four stars. The rating depends mostly on the number of services available, rather than the quality or cleanliness of the site:
    - 1-star sites have basic facilities (you may not get a hot shower),

    - 2-star sites should have a reception building, a shower block with hot water and maybe electrical hook-up,
    - 3-star sites should have multi-lingual reception staff, a shop, playground and maybe a swimming pool,
    - 4-star and 5-star sites are the most luxurious with private washing cubicles, communal cooking areas, at least one swimming pool, internet access and a café or restaurant.
- *www.searchforsites.co.uk* and *www.ukcampsite.co.uk* are both good databases of French campsites, with reviews in English.
- Check ahead whether your preferred site accepts dogs. Some have a cap on how many dogs you can have per pitch.
- Alan Rogers (*alanrogers.com*) focuses on the higher-end campsites and has reviews in English. You can either browse the website or buy books to read at your leisure.
- France has over 1,500 campsites in the ACSI CampingCard out-of-season scheme (*www.campingcard.co.uk/france*). To use this scheme, you buy a couple of books each year, which list out all the member sites across France and several other countries. One of the books has a pop-out card which you fill in the back of, and then simply present at reception when you book-in. There's also a digital version of the card with a QR code, which you can download to your phone and show to reception. The cards give you a fixed nightly price for two adults, one dog, a motorhome and electrical hook-up. Check the books for the nightly price and the dates when the discounts apply, as the definition of 'out-of-season' varies widely between sites.

- Some smaller site's reception may close for several hours at lunch. Check when reception is open before setting off, or you may find yourself sat around with a few other campers waiting to get in.
- Some sites close over the winter and spring, check before arriving.
- Although some staff may speak some English, it's best to assume folks at reception will only speak French, especially on smaller sites. Knowing a few words like these will get you by:
    - *Bonjour* (hello)
    - *Un camping-car* (one motorhome)
    - *Emplacement* (a pitch)
    - *Deux adultes* (two adults)
    - *Deux enfants* (two children)
    - *Trois nuits* (three nights)
    - *Avec électricité* (with electricity)
    - *Sans électricité* (without electricity)
    - *À l'ombre* (shaded)
    - *Merci* (thank you)

  For example, "Hello, I would like a pitch for my motorhome with electricity for two nights with two adults and a child" would be *"Bonjour, je voudrais un emplacement avec électricité pour mon camping-car pour deux nuits avec deux adultes et un enfant"*. Phonetically, this should sound something like this:

  "bon-sure, sher vood-dray un emplasser-mon
  por mon camping car avek electricitay por der nwee
  avek der adult ay un onfon".

- Some campsites offer a bakery service, where they'll source *croissants*, *pain-au-chocolat*, *baguettes* and so on and either hold them in reception in the morning, or some even deliver them to your van. You usually need to order the day before.
- You can't generally wear swimming shorts in French campsite pools (or any other French pools) but will have to wear Speedo type swimwear. The theory is these keeps the pools cleaner.
- Some sites charge a lot for pets, €5 a night per dog for example, or don't allow them at all. Best to check before you book or arrive.

The Aires Network

Once we'd discovered the French 'aires' network we didn't look back. These overnight parking areas are starting to appear in the UK, but there are a huge number in France. They are official places to stay, dedicated to motorhomes and are either maintained by the local authorities or by private individuals or companies.

A familiar sight across France, signs pointing to motorhome facilities

Aires tend to have much reduced facilities compared with campsites. They often have no formal 'pitch' area and more closely resemble a car park with larger-than-normal spaces. In fact, some aires are part of general car parks, just set to one side with signs and paint indicating which spots are for motorhomes and which are for cars.

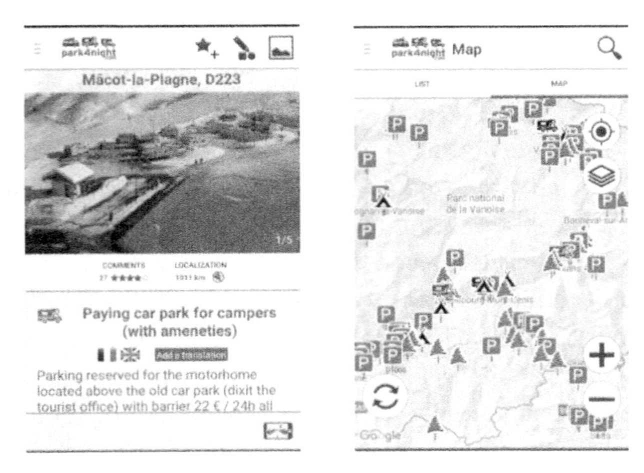

The park4night smartphone app and a listing for an aire

Here are some tips for finding great motorhome aires in France:

- There are several books which provide details of aires in France: GPS co-ordinates, nightly cost, a photo and so on. The best-known English language ones are 'All the Aires France' by Vicarious Media (*www.vicarious-shop.com*) and 'Camperstop Europe' by Facile Media (*www.facilemedia.eu*).
- There are, of course, websites and smartphone/tablet apps which detail French aires. The best known are *park4night* (which includes campsites and free camping locations), *campercontact.com* (which is only official aires and campsites) and *searchforsites* (campsites, aires and unofficial locations). We use *park4night* extensively, finding the multiple photographs and up-to-date user reviews are very helpful and easy to access using a smartphone app. You can also pay a few pounds and access all the *park4night.com* data offline.
- When looking for an aire, we often use the user-submitted review ratings to find the very best ones, looking for a relatively good score (4 or more out of 5 stars) from several reviews, ideally more than ten. That's just a rough rule of thumb though, we don't apply it rigorously, especially as some French motorhome tourists are particularly price-sensitive and will give some aires a poor rating simply because they deem them expensive.
- You can't book into aires (other than the Camping-Car Park ones described in the next section). They're first-come, first-served. Arriving between 11am and 2pm is a good tactic for getting a space at the busier aires. If you arrive and there is no space, there is sometimes 'overflow' parking nearby, otherwise you'll be expected to go and find another aire or a campsite.
- Aires are low-cost. Many are free, many charge around €10 to €18 a night, and the most expensive ones are around €25 to €30 a night. You usually pay using a machine on-site, some of which only take credit and debit cards. Sometimes the municipal police or someone else come around to collect payment in the morning or evening. They don't charge per person or for pets, just per motorhome.
- Many aires have time limits of between 24 hours and a few days. The rules are sometimes enforced by the local police, who may

come for a nightly look around the aire while doing their rounds, just to check all is well.

- Some aires have electrical hook-up available for some or all the pitches, but most don't. If electricity is available, it's usually unmetered and included in the nightly fee.
- Many aires have a service point for obtaining fresh water, dumping grey and black (WC) waste and sometimes hook-up for battery charging. These service points can be very busy in the morning at the more popular aires, so consider doing your servicing in the evening.
- Aires aren't restricted to French motorhomes. Any nationality of motorhome can use them, and you'll frequently see British, German, Belgian, Dutch, Italian and other countries represented.
- Only self-contained motorhomes can stay on aires, so you'll need a toilet on board. Caravans can't stay on French aires.
- Many aires restrict you to parking only, so you can't get your awning, chairs and table out for example, but you can use your ramps and open your windows. There is usually a sign telling you any rules, but some French motorhome travellers ignore this restriction, especially at lunchtime in hot weather.
- We've found aires to be safe places to stay and have never suffered a break-in on one. Some aires look safer than others though, and we exercise judgement on which ones we stay on overnight. As a rule, no-one recommends sleeping in motorway (*autoroute*) aires or rest areas as they have a poor reputation for thefts.
- Spaces can be tight up against each other in aires. Some have more room available than others, but more than once we've only just been able to open our door. Fingers crossed your neighbour doesn't snore.
- Aires aren't always the best choice in very hot weather, as few of them have any shade available and you might not be able to get your awning out to create shade.
- Try not to park door-to-door at aires. Space between vans is often limited, sometimes only a metre, and having doors on opposite sides increases privacy a little. So, if your motorhome has the door on the UK side, you may find yourself driving into a space while the motorhomes either side of you have reversed in.

Here are a few photos of aires we've stayed in, to give you an idea what they look like:

The motorhome aire near Capbreton

This typical French aire has no marked spaces, a gravel base and needs ramps (*les cales*) to get level.

The aire at Auris en Oisans La Station, which has a nightly rate and a season rate for the entire ski season.

Camping-Car Parks (PASS'ETAPES Card)

Camping-Car Parks are a kind of half-way house between campsites and aires (*www.campingcarpark.com*). They're a network of over 600 paid stopovers across France (with more in other countries), run by a single company. They typically cost between €13 and €18 a night. Some operate as campsites during the high season, closing their shower block in low season, reverting back to aires for self-contained vehicles.

Entrance to the Camping-Car Park at Morgat, Brittany

Unlike aires, you can book Camping-Car Parks before you arrive. You'll need to upgrade your membership to do so, by buying an annual PACK'PRIVILÈGES. You can also see real-time updates on how many free spaces there are at each aire, using a free smartphone app.

Some Camping-Car Parks include the cost of services such as electrical hook-up, WiFi, waste disposal and fresh water. Check the website or app for your planned stop before you visit or book. If you prefer a paper map, you can order it from their website, along with a free-to-download printable summary of each location.

To use any of the sites in the network you need to buy a PASS'ETAPES Card for €5. You can do this at any of their sites or order it through their website before leaving the UK. After that there are no fees other than your overnight costs. You can either pre-load your PASS'ETAPES Card or pay using a UK debit or credit card at a multilingual machine at the entrance to the site. If you experience any issues, there's a call centre you can contact which has English-speaking operatives, who we've found to be very helpful.

Free (Wild) Camping

There are so many campsites and aires in France that we don't normally bother trying to find free-camping (or wild-camping) places. That said, free-camping, which in this context means staying overnight in places which aren't formally designated for motorhomes, or are semi-official (tolerated parking), can be a great experience in France.

Free camping at the Col du Lautaret, just south of the Col du Galibier

As usual with free or wild-camping, discretion is needed to avoid upsetting locals or attracting the attention of the police. As these locations typically have no services available, you must plan to arrive with fresh water, and empty waste tanks. Leave no trace of your presence when you leave.

Coastal areas and protected parks are best avoided, as are areas outside official aires in towns. We've spent some memorable nights free camping in the Alps, with stupendous views of the mountains.

Don't park here, this sign means 'forbidden for motorhomes'

We tend to use the park4night app on our smartphones to find unofficial or semi-official places to stay. Others use Google Maps to seek out likely-looking areas or have bikes or a moped they use to scout out an area before moving their motorhome to their evening sleeping spot.

Pay-For Wild Camping: Evazion

Evazion is a new scheme managed by campsite group Huttopia *(evazion.co)*. It only has a small number of locations at present, offering the opportunity to formally book and pay to stay in unique off-grid wild-camping locations. If you like the idea of trying out wild camping but are worried about being moved on, this scheme is worth looking at.

The France Passion Scheme

Over 2,000 French businesses, typically restaurants, vineyards and farms, are part of the France Passion scheme. You join this scheme by buying a book each year, then you're welcome to spend a free night at any of the businesses listed in the book. You also get access to a smart phone app which maps the locations, lets you read reviews and so on.

There is no obligation to buy anything from the host business, just to say *bonjour* when you arrive and *au revoir* when you leave. You do need to be self-sufficient though, as most France Passion sites don't have toilets, showers or a motorhome service point available. As some locations are working farms, you also need to check the listings to ensure dogs are accepted, if you have one.

The France Passion book, map, app, card and sticker

We've really enjoyed the France Passion scheme over the years, staying on olive, lavender, snail and goat farms, vineyards, restaurants and *auberges* (a French word for an inn). Although there is no formal obligation to buy from the owners, we always buy something and we've been rewarded with some exceptional meals, cheese, olive oil and even fresh snails. If you speak some French, then these places are a wonderful low-pressure way to practice your language skills.

House Camping

Private houses across France (and wider Europe) encourage camping in their gardens or driveways in return for a fee. Hundreds advertise on websites like *www.homecamper.com* and offer a variety of services from simple parking to electrical hook-up, showers, breakfasts and WiFi. One big advantage of these places is access to knowledgeable locals who can help you get the most from the surrounding area.

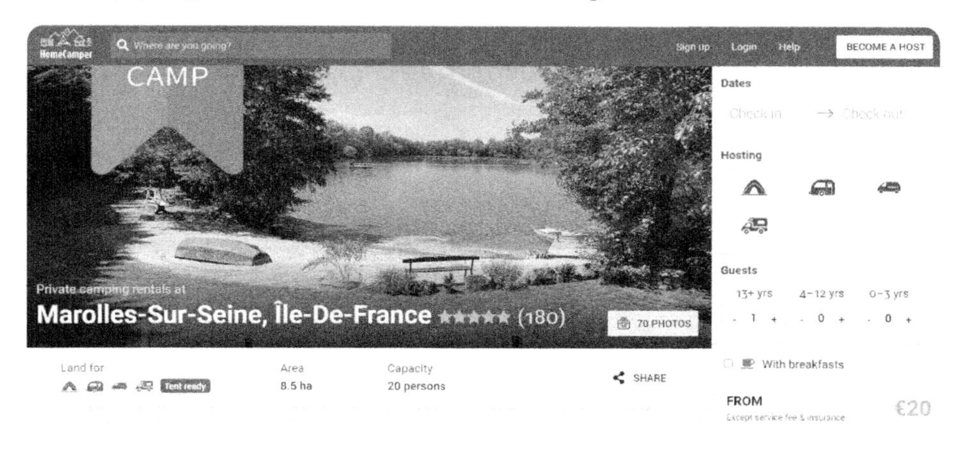

The HomeCamper website

Free Guidebooks for Places to Stay

While you're out and about in France keep an eye out for publications listing details of places to stay. We've picked up a couple of guides from tourist information, both for free:

- **Les 100 Plus Beaux Détours de France**. This lists out 100 places to visit across France, a great way to get inspiration for your travels. It also lists how many motorhome spaces are available. You can find the guide at tourist information at any of the included towns and villages, see the scheme's website for more information: *www.plusbeauxdetours.com*.

- **Les Villages Étapes en Camping Car**. This scheme includes villages which are a relatively short distance from fast, free roads and which specifically have a motorhome overnight parking area. See the scheme's website for more details: *www.village-etape.fr*.

Free guidebooks available for motorhome travellers in France

Stopovers Near the North France Ports

We tend to use Dunkirk and Calais when crossing to and from France, and usually spend our first and last nights within an easy drive of these ports. This section lists out a few of the places we've stayed in the past, just for an idea of some of the options available. They're all aires, but there are also lots of campsites available in the area.

We can also recommend the three-star Camping du Fort Lapin in **Calais** if you need a stop a short drive from the ferry or tunnel terminals (*camping-du-fort-lapin.fr*). The site is secure, near the beach, has English-speaking staff and has free public transport into Calais and to the Auchan hypermarket.

Free, official motorhome parking at Oye Plage

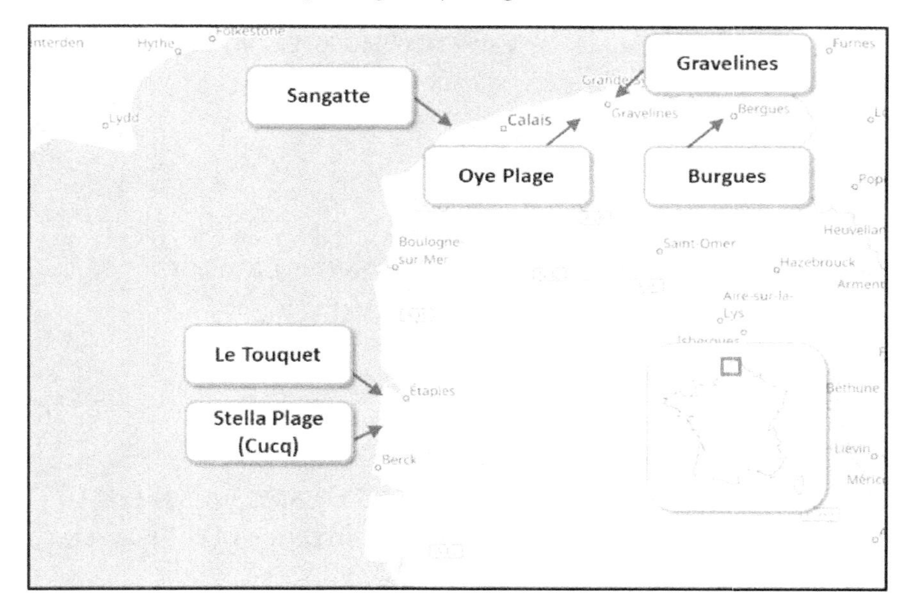

Here are some basic details for each of the aires shown on the map:

Gravelines

- 30 mins to Calais, 20 mins to Dunkirk
- Paid aire a short walk from the town (GPS: N50.98810, E2.12249), facing L'Aa canal with pleasure boats
- Paid service point a short drive away

Burgues

- 40 mins to Calais, 35 mins to Dunkirk
- Free 48 hours motorhome parking (GPS: N50.96524, E2.43610), short walk from town
- No services

Sangatte

- Only accessible to vans under 2.1m high
- 30 mins to Calais, 40 mins to Dunkirk
- Free motorhome parking (GPS: N50.94090, E1.74156)
- Short walk to the beach and countryside walks
- No services

Oye Plage

- 20 mins to Calais, 25 mins to Dunkirk
- Free motorhome parking (GPS: N50.97691, E2.03924)
- On edge of small town, drive or cycle to the beach
- Paid service point

Le Touquet

- 70 mins to Calais, 90 mins to Dunkirk
- Paid aire, relatively expensive (GPS: N50.535801, E1.593100)
- Close to a nautical centre, 30 min walk to centre of Le Touquet, short walk to beach and dunes
- Paid service point

Stella Plage (Cucq)

- 75 mins to Calais, 95 mins to Dunkirk
- Free aire, next to dunes, short walk to beach and town (GPS: N50.47412, E1.57727). Next to a campsite is the aire is full.
- Paid service point adjacent

Fresh Water & Waste (Bornes and Service Points)

France is peppered with motorhome service points, sometimes called *bornes*, where you can obtain fresh water, dump waste (grey) water, empty your toilet cassette (black waste) and sometimes recharge your leisure battery. Service points are often located in aires, but some are stand-alone, by the roadside, at petrol stations and supermarkets.

French service points are typically very well designed, with a large drive-over area to make it easier to get your grey waste pipe in the right place. They tend to have at least two taps: one for loading with fresh water or *eau potable* (drinking water), and one for rinsing your chemical toilet cassette. To try and avoid people getting these the wrong way around, the fresh water tap usually has a ¾" thread for a hosepipe connector, or a male to male type of hose connection, while the WC tap has no thread. You normally need your own hosepipe or water carrier.

As some folks do manage to get the two taps mixed up and use the fresh water one to rinse their loo, we wipe the water tap with an anti-bacterial wipe before we use it. Sometimes the toilet waste tap only works if you pay, in this case we use our grey water to rinse the cassette if we don't need to fill up with fresh water.

The motorhome service point at Stella Plage near Cucq on the Opal Coast. Dumping is free but fresh water and electricity are both paid at this borne.

At most service points you can dump grey and black waste for free, although one design has the black waste disposal in a cabinet, which you can't open without paying. Fresh water is sometimes free, but usually costs €3 to €5 for a 100 litre or 10 min flow. If mains electricity is available, it's roughly the same price for an hour of charge, although this is sometimes awkward to use as you may have to occupy the service point during charging, stopping other motorhomes accessing it.

Flot Bleu motorhome service point, the black waste emptying and fresh water hose are in the cabinet on the side of the far unit.

Paid service points mostly take cash, debit or credit cards (known as *Carte Bleue* or CB). A few require a smartphone app, with instructions posted on the service point. A handful still take tokens called *jetons*, which vary in design between bornes, and which you need to buy from a local shop, tourist office or from a machine like the Flot Bleu unit on the left in the above photo. A sign on the service point will tell you where to go to obtain a suitable jeton.

You lift the black cover at the bottom to dispose of your black waste, a button above it rinses the area. The tap for fresh water is on the other side.

Many service points will stop dispensing water in winter, at which time they may be marked *hors gel*. This is to protect them from freezing. The location of service points is marked on applications like park4night and campercontact, but it's the comments on these apps that may help you establish in advance whether fresh water is available in cold conditions. Otherwise, you just have to turn up and try, then move to another service point if the water is off. It makes sense to refill before you run out of water in winter unless you plan to visit campsites as you travel.

Obtaining and Using Euros

Our preference is to carry less than €100 of currency with us as cash, so we don't have to worry about theft. We don't normally buy Euros in the UK, but instead use the ATM cash machines in France to obtain cash, which all allow you to select your language once you insert your card. Be aware that some ATMs charge you to use them, it will usually tell you on the screen before it dispenses the cash giving you the chance to cancel the transaction. Most ATMs will also offer you the option of being charged in Euros or Pounds (and will show you the calculation). We always choose to be charged in Euros and let our bank sort out the currency exchange as their rate is always better than the ATM.

We have a Nationwide current account which (for a monthly fee) includes European breakdown cover and travel insurance. It doesn't charge us for transactions or using cash machines abroad. In the past we have also used a prepaid CaxtonFX currency card. We used to 'load' this with Euros by logging into the *caxtonfx.com* website and buy the amount of Euros we want to put on our card, fixing the exchange rate at that point. There are other similar prepaid currency cards available.

We also use a Halifax Clarity credit card which also doesn't charge a fee for using it abroad. However, it does charge interest on any cash withdrawals, which is why we use the Nationwide card for getting cash.

If you are planning on using a pre-paid credit card or normal bank account, it's worth knowing that self-service petrol stations 'pre-authorise' your card by ring-fencing an amount of money on it, usually around €100. They then also charge you for the fuel you buy. It can take up to a couple of weeks for the ring-fenced money to be released. With a bank account or pre-paid card, this can run up an overdraft or stop the card working even when there is still money on it, because it has all been ring-fenced. To stop this being an issue we use our credit card at fuel stations.

Coping with the Language

French people speak French. Some of them will speak English, especially the younger generations, but it's a safer bet to assume they won't, or they won't feel comfortable trying. Assuming, like us, you don't speak fluent French, then it's still not a huge issue. Much of your day-to-day life in France won't require much discourse with the locals, although it's great to be able to share a few words at least. Here are a few suggestions for how to handle the language barrier:

- Learn a few basic words. The French always greet each other with *bonjour* during the day, and *bon soir* in the evening (we've never worked out exactly what time they switch!). A *merci* (thankyou) always goes down well.
- If you have a smart phone, get a translation application like Google Translate. You can speak into this app and it will speak back the French translation out loud. You can even photograph a menu and

it will try to translate it for you, although the dish names may make no sense in English!

- If you need to ask if someone speaks English, we've found it best to ask if they speak *any* English, as otherwise they're fearful you'll expect them to be fluent: *vous parlez un peu anglais?* (*voo parlay un per arnglay?*) means "do you speak a little English?"

Finding Fuel in France

Diesel, unleaded petrol and LPG are widely available in France.

Buying Diesel and Petrol

At petrol stations you'll come across the following pumps (these are the usual colours, but they can vary so check carefully before filling):

- Black, orange or yellow handle: diesel, or *gazole*. Diesel is also labelled B7 or B10, with the numbers shown in a square. Stations sometimes sell premium diesel under a brand name like *Excellium*.
- Green handles: *sans plomb*, unleaded at either 95 or 98 octane. The latter is sometimes labelled *super*. Unleaded fuel is also shown as E5 or E10, with 5% or 10% biofuel, the numbers shown in a circle.
- Blue handle: *superethanol*, or E85, again shown in a circle.

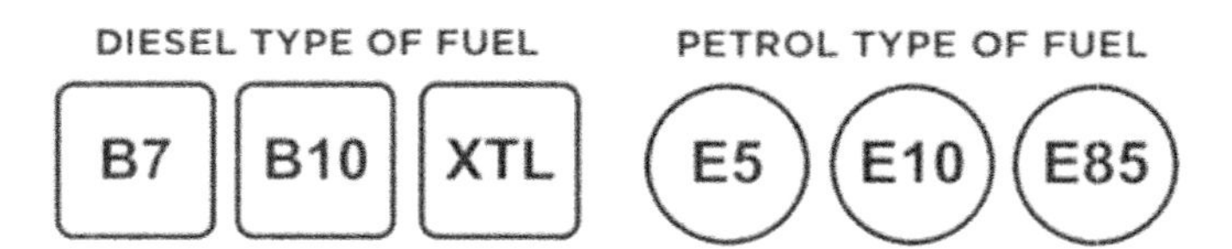

European standard fuel pump labels for diesel and petrol

Some fuel stations are manned, with someone in a small booth collecting payment as you leave. The payment window is usually too low to pay from the van window; it's easier if a passenger pays and gets back into the van after the driver has passed the barrier. Some stations have a mixture of self-payment and booth payment lanes. Some are 24 hours self-payment. Some switch to self-payment at night. They all take UK credit and debit cards. We tend to have at least two different cards from different issuers, just in case the station won't accept one of them though, and enough cash hidden in the van to cover the cost as a fall back.

Supermarket petrol stations in France are generally less expensive than the other brands. Look out for Carrefour, Intermarché, Super U or Auchan as you drive, or on your satnav points of interest. Various smart phone apps, like *Gaspal - Prix de l'essence*, show real-time fuel prices too, allowing you to spot the cheapest fuel around you or on your route.

In winter, we've been advised to buy diesel near to the mountains if we plan to drive into them. This is to help ensure the fuel has an anti-gel additive in it before we head into low temperature areas. An alternative would be to buy your own anti-gel fuel supplement and add it to the diesel tank yourself, following the instructions on the bottle.

Some French petrol stations are not easy to use in a motorhome as they are quite tight. On more than one occasion we've filled up and paid and then reversed out the entrance rather than try to drive through. We also once found ourselves wedged on top of a high plinth in a French petrol station as we tried to drive out, having to use a hammer to free our trapped exhaust. The self-service pumps are usually less tight than the 'pay at the booth' pumps. We now try and look at a fuel station before driving in, and if it looks like it might be too awkward, we head elsewhere.

Buying Gas (LPG, Butane and Propane)

You can't get UK Calor or Flogas bottles refilled in France (or anywhere else outside the UK). You have a few choices to ensure you have enough gas while on your trip to France:

1. Take enough **Calor Gas** or **Flogas** with you for your full journey. The amount of gas you'll need will depend mainly on whether you use it for air heating. A 6kg bottle might easily last two or three weeks with no heating on, or just a few days if it's on day and night.
2. Fit at least one **Campingaz** cylinder and pigtail/regulator. You can buy replacement Campingaz bottles in France and several other countries (*www.campingaz.com* has a map of sales locations). If you choose this option be aware that Campingaz cylinders are relatively small and expensive, plus they're mostly butane so aren't suitable for temperatures close to or below 0°C (look for ones which are a butane/propane blend).

3. Buy a **French bottle** from a petrol station, for example. You'll need a size which fits in your locker (they're generally 13kg or 5kg/6kg, depending on whether they have propane or butane), and you'll have to pay a deposit and sign a contract when you get the bottle (use the address of a local French campsite if you need one). You'll also need the correct French pigtail for the type of bottle you buy (the high-pressure pipe which connects the bottle to your bulkhead regulator) or a connection adapter. You can buy these from hardware shops like Leroy Merlin if you haven't already bought one before you leave the UK. One advantage of this method is that you can keep your place in ski aires or on a campsite, if they sell gas bottles on-site.
4. Fit one or more **Self-Refillable LPG** bottles or a tank to your motorhome. With these you can visit one of hundreds of LPG stations and refill the bottle(s) yourself. LPG is sometimes labelled GPL or Autogas in France, and you need a special type of gas bottle or tank fitted to your van to use it. These systems have a cut-off built in so they can't be filled to more than 80% capacity. The main options are Safefill (*safefill.co.uk*), Alugas (*www.alugas.eu*) and Gaslow (*www.gaslowdirect.com*).

The European standard label for LPG, among other gaseous fuels

If you choose to fit a self-refillable LPG system, here are a few hints for using it in France, based on our experience:

- France uses the dish-shaped LPG adapter shown below. You'll need one of these. The UK's 'bayonet' LPG adapter won't fit in France.

- Usually, LPG can only be bought when the station is manned. That means you can't generally fill up in the late evening or overnight. In some places you can't fill on Sundays or at lunchtime either.
- We have a dual-bottle system with one 11kg and one 6kg bottle, with an auto-changeover valve. This is enough for several weeks, maybe two months in summer, or a week or two in deep cold, with the gas powering the heating day and night. The auto-changeover valve changes colour when we switch to our 6kg bottle, at which point we look for somewhere to fill the 11kg one.

Our dual-bottle self-refillable LPG system

- Websites like *mylpg.eu* map out LPG stations but be aware they're not always accurate.
- If you're passing close to Luxembourg, LPG is very cheap there and the same price in all motorway service stations.
- There's a continual debate on motorhome forums on whether some French filling stations will refuse to allow motorhomes to fill

gas cylinders, even ones which are designed for safe self-refills (with a built-in 80% cut-off). We opted to fit an external refill point to avoid having to open the gas locker, as this is supposed to reduce the risk of refusal and have only once been refused a refill. That particular station was closing for lunch at the time, which could have been the more likely explanation.

Often the LPG pump at French filling stations is only accessible from one side. If it's not on the side of our refill point, we can normally still get the hose around to the other side with some shuffling around.

Eating Well in France

France and Italy fight it out for the title of Gastronomic Champion of Europe. Somehow the French seem to be able to take pretty much any ingredient and make it taste out-of-this-world. Even if you're not planning to eat out in the enormous range of restaurants and cafés available, you'll still have the opportunity to try out lots of new foodstuffs available from supermarkets and street markets.

Supermarkets

France has a very good range of supermarkets available. We mix up our shopping between the budget brands (there are around 1,500 Lidl stores and 900 ALDI shops in France) and the more expensive shops, which have a wider range, plus some street market shopping. We don't really have any favourite supermarkets, we just pick whichever tends to be on our route or nearby, looking out for these names: Intermarché, Auchan, Super U, Carrefour and E. Leclerc.

High Street Shopping

Most French villages and towns still have at least one bakers (*boulangeries*), cake shop (*patisseries*) and butchers (*boucheries*) on the high street. They can be a little intimidating, but we find if we let them know we're English (*anglaise*, pronounced *arn-glay*), the staff are helpful and friendly, and we can get away with our poor French skills. Worst case, we point at what we want and hold up the number of fingers for how many we want.

Markets and Street Food

Fresh fruit and vegetables, oils, fish, meat, nuts, cheese, cooked chickens, speciality foods, you name it, it's all available on the many street markets which take place across France. As well as the opportunity to stock up your fridge and cupboards, these markets are a great place to observe French country life taking place, as the locals come together and use them as social gatherings.

www.jours-de-marche.fr has a list of market days in France. The website is in French but you can use Google Translate (*translate.google.com*) to render it into English.

French street markets often sell roast chickens

Fresh oysters for sale in St Malo

Eating Out

Our top tip for eating out in France is to keep an eye out for a lunchtime *menu du jour*. These are typically three-course meals served between around 12 and 2pm for about €18 to €28 a head. They can be very popular, as the restaurant or café fills up with locals and folks working nearby.

Why not take a break and enjoy a mid-day meal in the sun?

Menus are usually limited to a couple of choices for each course and are almost always in French. Even if your language skills are OK, descriptions for meals are often indecipherable! We take a menu translator with us, which is in some guidebooks, or failing that accept this as part of the fun, and we share two options from the menu.

Staying in Touch in France

It's never been easier to stay in touch with family, friends and the wider world while you're abroad.

Using the Internet

The easiest way to access the internet in France is to use your phone or a personal WiFi hotspot device (sometimes called a MiFi or a router), with a UK SIM card. To do this:

- Before leaving the UK, check with your SIM provider that you can use your phone abroad and what you need to do to keep your roaming costs low (you may need to buy a 'bundle' of data, for example).
- You'll need to turn on data roaming on your phone or MiFi. This will enable it to access the internet outside the UK. Once abroad your phone will connect to the best available foreign network, so it doesn't matter which network your SIM is on in the UK.
- If you have a 5G-capable phone or router, fellow travellers are now reporting widespread availability of these fast networks across France.
- Most UK providers cap the amount of data you can use in the EU to between 12GB and 50GB a month. We don't work online while away. If we stream a few hours of internet TV a day, we find we need around 100GB a month, otherwise we tend to use about 30GB to 40GB a month. If you need more data than your phone SIM offers abroad, we suggest checking the Money Saving Expert website for the latest situation on data roaming SIM cards: *www.moneysavingexpert.com/mobiles/cheap-roaming-calls*.
- You can buy a pay-as-you-go SIM card in France to get more data than UK providers will offer. You don't need a French address or French bank account to do this, you can pay with your UK credit or debit card. Take a passport with you when you go to the shop to buy the SIM. This website is useful for getting the latest information on French SIMs: *prepaid-data-sim-card.fandom.com/wiki/France*.
- If you need 200GB of roaming data a month (which covers other EU countries, not just France), we've had several recommendations for Spanish provider TIEKOM. All this data can be used in France and across the EU, and they'll post the SIM card to the UK (*tiekom.com/internet-at-home/data-sim*).
- An issue with foreign SIM cards is they're blocked by BBC iPlayer and many other UK streaming services. To get around this you can pay for software called a VPN, which you'd usually install on your streaming TV stick, laptop and/or smartphone. This site covers the best ones available: *www.techradar.com/vpn/best-vpn*. Some providers offer a 30-day free trial, which could cover you for your entire holiday.

- If you have a UK contract, ask your SIM provider to cap the monthly amount of money you're able to spend. Even if you have a high monthly allowance, it's quite possible to use more, especially if you watch a lot of TV or films. This can result in a large bill when you return home.
- If you're using a router to connect to the internet (a personal WiFi hotspot for example), and it refuses to connect when you insert a new SIM, check the APN settings on the router. These need to be correct for the SIM to work. Ask your network provider what the APN settings should be or search their website and check your router's user guide for how to amend the APN settings.
- Another option to cellular (3G, 4G and 5G) networks is to use WiFi. This is typically available at campsites, cafés and restaurants. WiFi networks don't limit how much you can download or upload and are often free when you purchase something from the establishment, but you may have to ask for password or the *clé wifi* (pronounced *clay wee fee*). If you use these, avoid accessing any sensitive websites like internet banking unless you're using a VPN, as the networks might not be secure.
- Companies like *motorhomewifi.com* sell specialised motorhome internet boosters and SIM cards and are worth talking to if you're not sure about what you'll need.

We use a 4G Huawei personal WiFi hotspot router which has a SIM card in it. It connects to the internet, and shares this to our phones, laptops and other devices using a private wireless network. It displays the total data used by all our devices on the front, which is very helpful for tracking our overall use. If you want to future-proof your kit, the 5G ZTE MU5001 is worth a look, and can be connected to an external antenna. As an alternative to using a MiFi router, you can often use a smartphone to create a WiFi hotspot. Sharing a SIM card connection in this way is called *tethering,* most SIM suppliers allow it, but not all.

Making Phone Calls

The easiest way to make phone calls or send text messages from France is to use your mobile phone with your UK SIM in it. To call a UK number, add 0044 (or +44) to the start and remove the leading 0 for example

07123 456 789 becomes +44 7123 456 789. To call a French number from a UK mobile, you need to add the numbers 0033 (or +33) to the start of the French number and again remove the leading 0. Check with your UK SIM provider whether they have any packages to reduce the cost of making calls abroad.

Alternatively, if you have a smartphone with data roaming turned on, you can use internet phone calls or video calls with applications like Facebook, Skype and WhatsApp. Remember to check your data allowance before you do this.

Watching TV

We use a combination of methods to watch TV when we're in France:

- **Satellite TV** - we have a roof-mounted satellite dish and a 12V TV which has a built-in Freesat decoder, which gives us the free-to-air Freesat channels. We can watch TV across all of France with this set-up, although not if there's a tree in the way or if it's windy!
- **Internet TV** - we have an Amazon Fire TV Stick device which allows us to stream TV using the Internet. Some channels are restricted to the UK, so can't be watched abroad without a VPN although we find they're often accessible if we use a UK-registered SIM.
- **iPlayer Downloads** - if we download them while we're in the UK, we can watch iPlayer programs and films when we're abroad for about a month. We can either watch them on our laptop or connect the laptop to our TV with a HDMI cable. This saves us using our data allowance when abroad.
- **DVDs** - our TV has a built-in DVD player, so we buy DVDs from charity shops before we leave.

Sending and Receiving Post

Postcards might be old-fashioned these days, but everyone still loves getting them! We buy stamps from a *tabac*, the French equivalent of a UK newsagent. You can also go to a post office, but their hours are often short, and queues long. We take the postcard with the UK address already written on it, so the tabac staff can see it's for the UK (*Grande Bretagne* or *Royaume-Uni*; Ireland is either *Eire* or *Irland*) and ask for a *timbre* (pronounced *tarm-brer*). French post boxes are yellow, and some have a dedicated slot for post to be sent abroad, labelled *étranger*.

It's also possible to get post sent to you at a French post office, by using the *poste restante* service. There's more information about the service here: *www.postoffice.co.uk/mail/poste-restante*. We've used this service a few times and find it best used for low value items, as it's not 100% reliable. We have also had post delivered to campsites, but if the post is delayed you may have to stay there for some time.

If you can buy what you need from *amazon.fr* (the French version of Amazon), you can request delivery to an Amazon locker on your route. These are widespread across France. We've used this approach in Spain and it worked very well, with quick delivery and easy parcel pick-up. There are other brands of automated pick-up locker available too, in post offices and train stations for example. Check the delivery options for whichever online retailer you use.

Doing Your Laundry

If you're away for just a week or two you may not need to do any laundry; it may be the last thing on your mind when you're on holiday! However, if you do need to wash some of your gear, there are plenty of places to do it without resorting to hand-washing.

Campsite Laundries

If you plan to stay on a campsite, they usually have a washing machine (a *machine à laver*) and sometimes a dryer (a *sèche-linge*) too. You'll usually need your own washing detergent (*lessive*) and softener (*adoucissant*), but if you forget it the campsite shop may stock them. Campsites also have the advantage of allowing you to hang your washing out to dry, avoiding the cost of a dryer, in good weather at least. Remember to pack a clothes line and pegs if you plan to do this!

Self-Service Laundrettes

France has a good network of self-service launderettes. Search for *laverie automatique* and the name of the town and Google will oblige with a map of all the launderettes, so you can work out which is open, and the easiest to park near or carry your laundry bags to. Many are shown on the park4night app.

They have a payment machine where you select the number corresponding to the washer or dryer your clothes are in, and then pay. Take a stash of one and two-Euro coins with you, as the machines don't always take cards or give change. Sometimes washing detergent is included, or you can buy a dose of it from another machine in the laundry if you don't have your own.

Supermarkets

It feels a bit weird at first, but you can often wash and dry your clothes in supermarket car parks or even petrol stations in France. They have washers and dryers where you pop your washing in and wait in your motorhome, or go and do your shopping, while it washes. Timers give an idea when the washing will be ready to swap into the drier (some will even send you a text message). We've used these a lot and they usually have a machine which will take a large load such as duvets or all your washing in one go. You can find them on the park4night or Wash.ME apps, or search for Revolution-branded sites here: *stores.revolution-laundry.com*.

Washing our clothes in a supermarket car park

Tips for Handing Extreme Weather

While France isn't far from the UK, you might occasionally experience some relatively extreme weather conditions. On our tours we've seen temperatures in France as low as -10°C and as high as 35°C, although we should stress these were only on very rare occasions. Over the years we've learned a few tricks for coping with the weather, and we've shared them in the following sections.

Hot Weather Tips

In the event of being hit by a heatwave while you're away, here are a few tips for keeping your cool:

- Get your van under shade. If you can find a campsite with trees or man-made shade, then your van will stay much cooler.
- Create airflow. Open your windows and skylights. If we're on a campsite we often feel safe enough to leave windows open, at least partially, at night too.
- Put your awning out. If you have a roll out awning, use it to create shade on the side of your motorhome that is facing the sun.
- Fit thermal windscreen covers. If you have thermal cab window covers (like those from *www.silverscreens.co.uk*), putting them on can help your van stay cooler by deflecting the sun's heat.
- Shade your windows. We peg a towel onto the open side windows, to stop sunlight entering the van but still allow any breeze to flow.
- If you're near mountains, get to higher altitude. The higher you get the cooler it gets. On 2,000m mountain passes it can be very comfortable while it's roasting in the valleys below.
- Shade the fridge. Our fridge can cope until the temperature gets into the low 30°Cs, and then starts to warm up. We find it helps to park so that the sun doesn't shine onto the side of the van where the fridge is fitted. If we can't do this, we try to create some shade with fabric attached to our bike rack and wrapped around the fridge area (ensuring the vents aren't obstructed). Some people fit a fan inside the top fridge vent, but we've never tried this.
- If your van has cab air conditioning, consider driving in the early afternoon when the air is hottest, using the air con to keep cool.

- Consider buying an air conditioning unit. You can get units which hang over a side window if you don't want to fit one to the roof, or don't have space for one (*www.coolmycamper.com*). In our experience, other types of system, which don't run on mains electricity don't cool the van down much.

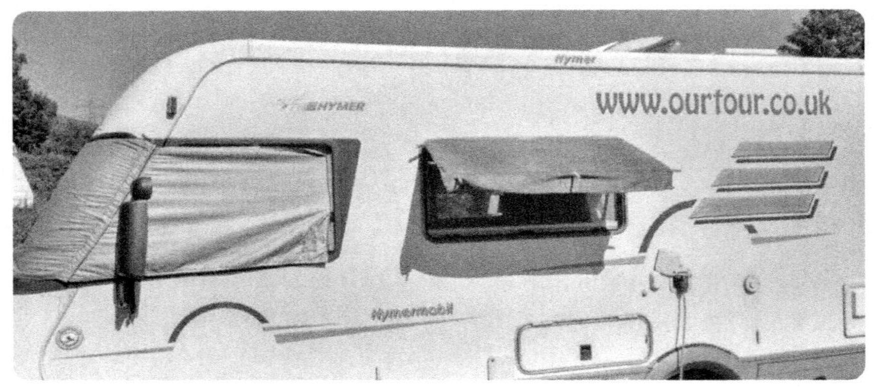

Our motorhome set up for handling a heatwave

Cold Weather and Ski Resort Tips

Heading into the mountains at any time can be a wonderful experience in a motorhome, but it tends to get a little chilly up there! In winter it's quite possible to tour resorts skiing or snowboarding, while staying in your motorhome in perfect comfort throughout. Winter campsites (sometimes called *caravaneige*) are usually on the ski bus route and offer heated boot rooms to dry out your kit. Have a browse around *www.campercontact.com* to get an idea of the types of winter parking area available. Many have wellness spas and some even have a heated bathroom on each pitch.

Ice on our motorhome at a French ski resort

Our experience of very cold weather touring has been limited to spending just a few days in aires high up in the Alps, but we quickly learned a bunch of things we were getting wrong! Here are a few pointers if you plan to head up into the snow and ice:

- Fit full winter tyres (marked with the 3PMSF mountain snowflake symbol) before setting off.
- Get a set of snow chains or socks for your driving wheels, and practice fitting the fiddly things before you need them for real. Don't put them on unless the road is covered in snow or ice. There are special *aire de chaînage* areas by the road where you can pull in to fit chains.
- To avoid your diesel gelling up (resulting in your engine not starting in the deep cold) try and top up with fuel from a station which is near the mountains. If needs be, ask if it has anti-gel additive in it. If you're concerned, buy and take some diesel winter fuel additive.
- Check when the local school holidays are: if you arrive just after they've started, you may find there is no room at the inn, or every electrical hook-up point has a full complement of cables.
- Get external silver screens for your cab windows to keep ice off, and try and keep some of the heat in.
- If your van doesn't have one fitted, carry a ladder and brush. You'll need to clear your roof of fresh snow, or it'll build into a thick ice sheet which might cause an accident when it comes off.
- Take a shovel. Aires may be cleared by snow ploughs, but they can't get to the area between vans. Each morning experienced winter motorhomers clear around their van to stop the snow building up.

- With temperatures dipping at night to -10°C or -15°C, and not getting above freezing during the day, you'll need your air and water heating on all day and night. Make sure your gas tanks are full, unless you're using a local bottle which might be available in-resort. You can get through 2 or 3kg of gas per 24 hours in deep cold. Butane won't work below freezing, so either use Propane or LPG. We have two bottles with an auto-changeover valve, so we don't have to get up at 2am to switch bottles when one runs out.
- Make sure you can either hook-up or your leisure batteries are full as you'll need electricity to run the heating fan all night. You can't guarantee solar PV charging when your panel keeps getting snowed on. Some folks use generators in ski resorts during the day to recharge leisure batteries. Winter sites tend to charge per amp hour, so electrical heating can prove expensive compared with gas.
- Be prepared for stuff freezing up: windscreen wipers, external locker locks, door hinges, your ramps freezing to the floor, ice building up on any flattish surface, you name it. One fellow traveller reported their awning being forced away from the side of their van by a build-up of ice.
- If your grey tank isn't winterised, open the tap and leave a bucket under it to catch the water as it comes out. Ideally fit tank heaters and insulation to any water tanks slung under your van.
- Take some pegs with you to keep your wipers off the windscreen. Attaching one to your heating exhaust outlet will mean any water condensing from it will freeze away from the side of your van.

If you are thinking of heading for the slopes in your motorhome the Motorhomes & Snow Facebook Group has lots of useful information, as does the *winterised.com* website.

Windy Weather Tips

If high winds are forecast, you can do some preparation to make life as comfortable and safe as you can in your van:

- Find a parking place which has some shelter, next to a building or in between other motorhomes, to take the brunt of the wind.
- If you have steadies, wind them down. We have these on the back of our van and while they don't stop all movement, they make it more comfortable to sleep during gusts of wind.

- Be careful opening doors and windows. We've twice snapped door hinges in windy weather.
- Check your parking area for anything which might get blown onto it, such as trees and signs, and consider moving if needs be. We once spent a sleepless night being chased around a car park by wind-driven bins on wheels!

Staying Safe and Dealing with Problems

France is a safe country to travel to and tour by motorhome. The roads are very good quality, the French are good drivers and break-ins and thefts are rare. That said, nowhere is 100% safe, and problems like break-downs do occur. This section provides some advice to keep your tour of France as safe and enjoyable as possible.

Driving Safety

Our number one, top tip for driving safely in France is this: **take your time**. Don't be pressurised into going more quickly than you feel comfortable. Driving on the right, on unfamiliar roads with the occasional unusual road sign or situation cropping up can be both exciting and wearing. We've only had one accident in years of driving in France which was just a clipping of wing mirrors. There are a few more tips we can share from our experience which might help you:

- Most road signs are similar to those used in the UK. The RAC (*www.rac.co.uk*) and AA (*theaa.com*) websites both have useful online guides to French signs and driving conditions, which only take a minute to read and may help avoid a problem abroad.
- Indicate early, especially when overtaking cyclists. The French love to cycle, they're completely mad when the Tour de France comes to town and cycle all-year round. When we come across a cyclist, or any other obstacle which will force us across to the left, we start to indicate very early. This helps ensure any cars or motorbikes behind us know not to overtake us just as we start to pull out.
- We find having the cab passenger navigating and 'spotting' for road signs is very useful to reduce the stress on the driver and to help get the motorhome into the correct lane at the right time.

- At STOP signs, you must come to a halt and pause before driving over the line. Some STOP signs are in unusual places, like on the main street through a village, forcing you to give way to traffic from a side street.
- Keep an eye on your speedo or on your satnav speed indicator. Rural France has lots of very long stretches of road with an 80kph (50mph) limit, and it's very easy to let your speed drift upwards.
- Remember *priorité à droite*, and the advice about using engine braking in the mountains, described earlier in this book.

Parking Safety

Whenever we would to get close to our destination, even if we'd never been there before, our dog Charlie would know and start barking. How did he know? We can only assume he could detect our stress levels rising! We're fairly relaxed when driving across France these days but clearly, we still get a little on-edge parking up! Perhaps because we use aires a lot, and we're never 100% sure there will be a space, but also the act of getting a big lumbering vehicle like a motorhome into a space and level on the ramps can be a mini-trial, especially after a long drive.

The difficulty in parking is no more than it would be in the UK and is sometimes much less as there's much more parking space in France. Supermarket car parks tend to be huge, at least outside of city centres, and motorhomes often park to one side, taking up a couple of spaces.

Other parking places are sometimes a tighter affair, so one of us gets out of the van to help the driver, with a series of hand signals we've worked out to say: 'go left', 'go right', 'come straight back', 'stop' and 'go forwards'. We've given up trying to shout instructions over the noise of the engine.

Personal Safety

There is already loads of travel advice in books like the Lonely Planet or Rough Guide series for staying safe when out on foot in unfamiliar places abroad. We won't try and repeat it all here, but lots of it is common sense and stuff you would do at home too:

- Even if we have them, we don't wear expensive clothes, jewellery or watches when out and about.

- We carry only small amounts of cash.
- We expect pick-pockets in very busy places and don't put anything in our back pockets. When it gets very busy, we walk with our hands on our purse/wallet/phone in our front pockets, zip them into an inside pocket, or carry them at the bottom of a rucksack.
- We carry a 'fake wallet' in places we're particularly cautious of, like underground tube stations or very busy markets. We fill an old wallet with receipts and low value coins and place it in the top of a backpack, so it's the first thing a thief sees if they open the bag.
- If we're concerned, we ask locally which areas might be best avoided. In France we only really worry about this in larger cities and at night time.

Finally, you may have come across stories of people being 'gassed' in their motorhomes when in Europe. Typically, they go like this: the victims wake up feeling groggy to find someone has been inside their motorhome during the night and stolen some of their belongings. The conclusion they come to is some sort of sleeping gas has been injected into the van to knock them out. Please, please, please do your research before you let these stories put you off. Not a single one of them has ever been verified by the police. When consulted, anaesthesiologists report it would be very expensive and incredibly difficult to safely knock out people in this way. In other words: it's a myth. The unfortunate victims slept through a professional burglary. You can best protect yourself with good locks, alarms and choosing safe places to sleep.

Contacting the Police in a Non-Emergency

If you need to report an issue to the police which requires them to come quickly, such as an issue with violence or robbery, call 17 from your phone. In the event of a non-emergency, look up the location of the local police station or gendarme and go there to file a complaint (search *www.service-public.fr* for '*porter plainte*').

Finding Medical Help if You Need It

Apart from needing to seek out vets in various countries, we've been lucky and haven't needed much medical help abroad. We both have EHICs (European Health Insurance Cards - these are being phased out and replaced with GHICs which do a similar job). We also buy travel insurance which includes cover for repatriation. Whenever we've needed long-term medication, we talk to our doctors to ensure we can take enough with us to cover the entire time away.

If we need medical help and it's not an emergency, we normally head for a pharmacy, campsite reception or tourist information to ask for advice. Failing that, we search the internet for local dentists, opticians or doctors. According to *about-france.com*: "The [EHIC] card gives access to treatment by doctors, dentists, and in public hospitals, or private clinics operating within the French "sécurité sociale" (health service) framework". The EHIC and replacement GHIC won't cover the full cost of medical treatment though, so we still take out travel insurance.

In the event of an emergency, and there was no-one we could quickly ask around us, we would call our travel insurers to get help. Having a local map handy at this point would probably be essential: *maps.me* and (the very similar) *Organic Maps* are great smartphone apps, or Google Maps is very good if you have internet access. Doctors surgeries are called *cabinets*, hospitals are called *hôpitals*, CHR (*Centre Hospitalier Régional*) or CHU (*Centre Hospitalier Universitaire*). A&E departments are called *urgences*. Failing that we would contact the French emergency services on 112, this will work from a UK mobile.

In the event of a mental health problem, you can call SOS Help, who have a helpline for English speakers in France, call 00 33 146 21 46 46 from a UK phone. You can also get online advice here: *soshelpline.org*.

Making Minor Repairs Abroad

If something minor breaks on your motorhome, then depending on your skill level and tools available, you have the option of fixing some stuff yourself. For simple fixes, there are DIY shops all over the place, look for names such as Leroy Merlin or Bricomarché, selling Gaffa Tape, super glue, screws and fibre glass. We tend to carry stuff like this in our tool kit, along with cable ties.

For minor engine repairs (we've fixed a diesel leak and a minor radiator leak while abroad), there are plenty of motor factors knocking about selling spares. Norauto and Feu Vert in France are the equivalent of Halfords (*norauto.fr* and *feuvert.fr*). Hardware shops (*bricolage*) can also be helpful, and supermarkets tend to sell a range of glues, fuses, bulbs and so on.

We also carry a spare wheel, brace, tyre pressure gauge and foot pump. We check our tyre pressures from time to time to ensure we're not losing air.

If you need something for your habitation area, then a motorhome dealer is your best bet. Just search the internet for *campingcar* and the name of the nearest big town and any dealers will be listed. Alternatively, ask around fellow motorhome owners in aires and campsites, or check the campsite shop for spares. Our water pump died near Annecy once and we found a dealer and replaced it within a couple of hours. Our fridge stopped working on gas, and we also managed to lose our main skylight on another trip, which were both replaced on a Friday afternoon for a reasonable price by a dealer's workshop (their *atelier*). If you need a part specific to your make of motorhome, they may have dealers in France who can help. We have a Hymer, for example, and there is a network of workshops mapped out on *hymer.com*.

Handling Breakdowns

With a well-serviced motorhome, you shouldn't break down while you're away. If you're unlucky and you do break down while you're in France, you've these options:

- If you have breakdown cover, call them and get them to come and try to fix the issue on the roadside, or recover you to a local garage. If the cover includes a hire car or overnight stays in a hotel, this can be the best option even if you could deal with the issue yourself. However, you can't call out your recovery company if you're on a French motorway. Instead, you need to use one of the orange emergency telephones, positioned every 2km along the motorway to call for help. If you can't do this, call 112, the emergency number from your mobile. A local recovery truck will take you from the motorway (which you will need to pay for, and reclaim from your breakdown company) and you can then call your UK recovery company to get you to a garage. The cost for vehicles under 3,500kg is fixed, but is higher between the hours of 18:00 and 08:00, weekends and bank holidays. The cost for vans over 3,500kg is not fixed.

- If you don't have breakdown cover, or the issue isn't critical and you want to sort it yourself, find a local garage. You can either take to the internet and start searching for one or ask someone who lives locally, tourist information or campsite reception. Our satnav has a 'Find Help' function which lists nearby garages, which we've found hit-and-miss, but better than nothing.
- For Fiat-based motorhomes, you can search for a local garage using this site: *www.fiatcamper.com*. Don't assume a main dealer will be able to see you quickly though, we've visited two on separate occasions which couldn't even look at the van for 10 days!

Mechanics don't tend to speak English but do tend to be a helpful bunch. Having an app like Google Translate on your smartphone (with either an offline language downloaded or internet access), or using the full Google Translate website (*translate.google.co.uk*) on their computer, is a slow method of communicating but is far better than pointing and mime.

Driving our motorhome onto a breakdown truck near Chartres

When driving on and off breakdown trucks, make sure the driver is aware of the risk of the back end grounding out. The flatbed truck sent to us only just allowed our 6m-long motorhome to drive onto it and needed two thick planks of wood under the rear wheels to keep the motorhome frame from scraping on the floor.

One final note: if your motorhome has broken down by the side of the road, refer to the advice below on using your yellow vests and warning triangle to help you stay safe.

Handling a Road Traffic Accident

In the unlikely event you're involved in an accident while in France, it might be simple enough to sort out, depending on how serious the incident was. As an initial response, you need to do this:

- Wear your yellow jackets if you're around other traffic
- Place your warning triangle a distance (30m say) behind your vehicle to warn other traffic
- Stand somewhere safe, behind a barrier if possible
- Call your insurer on your mobile phone

In our years of touring we've only had one minor accident in France. The other vehicle's driver produced a *constat à l'amiable* form which we both completed and sent to our insurers, although no claim was ever made on either side.

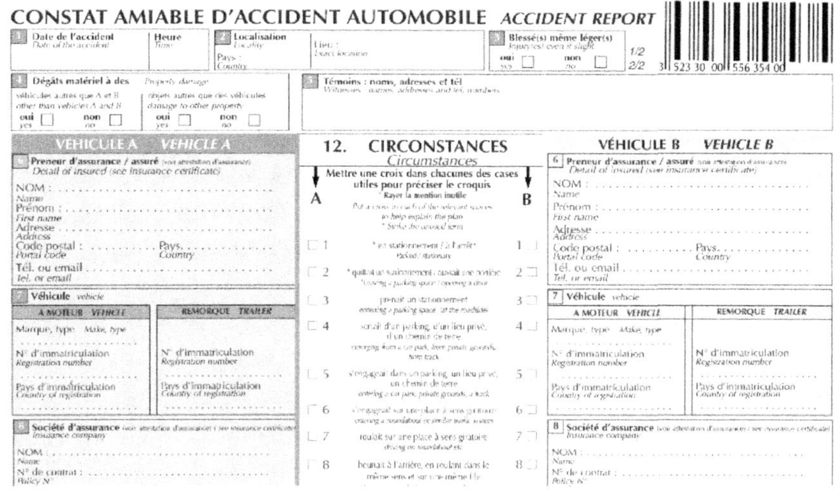

CONSTAT AMIABLE D'ACCIDENT AUTOMOBILE *ACCIDENT REPORT*

3 523 30 00 556 354 00

1/2
2/2

1 Date de l'accident / *Date of the accident* — Heure / *Time*

2 Localisation / *Locality* — Pays : / *Country* — Lieu : / *Exact location*

3 Blessé(s) même léger(s) / *Injury(es) even if slight* — oui / *yes* ☐ non / *no* ☐

4 Dégâts matériel à des / *Property damage*
véhicules autres que A et B / *other than vehicles A and B* — oui / *yes* ☐ non / *no* ☐
objets autres que des véhicules / *damage to other property* — oui / *yes* ☐ non / *no* ☐

5 Témoins : noms, adresses et tél / *Witnesses: names, addresses and tel. numbers*

VÉHICULE A *VEHICLE A*

6 Preneur d'assurance / assuré (voir attestation d'assurance) / *Detail of insured (see insurance certificate)*
NOM : / *Name*
Prénom : / *First name*
Adresse / *Address*
Code postal : / *Postal code* — Pays. / *Country*
Tél. ou email / *Tel. or email*

7 Véhicule *vehicle*

A MOTEUR *VEHICLE*	REMORQUE *TRAILER*
Marque, type *Make, type*	
N° d'immatriculation *Registration number*	N° d'immatriculation *Registration number*
Pays d'immatriculation *Country of registration*	Pays d'immatriculation *Country of registration*

8 Société d'assurance (voir attestation d'assurance) (see insurance certificate) / *Insurance company*
NOM : / *Name*
N° de contrat : / *Policy N°*

12. CIRCONSTANCES
Circumstances

Mettre une croix dans chacunes des cases utiles pour préciser le croquis
* Rayer la mention inutile
Put a cross in each of the relevant spaces to help explain the plan
* *Strike the unused term*

A		B
☐ 1	* en stationnement / à l'arrêt — *Parked / stationary*	1 ☐
☐ 2	* quittait un stationnement / ouvrait une portière — *leaving a parking space / opening a door*	2 ☐
☐ 3	prenait un stationnement — *entering a parking space / at the roadside*	3 ☐
☐ 4	sortait d'un parking, d'un lieu privé, d'un chemin de terre — *emerging from a car park, from private grounds, from track*	4 ☐
☐ 5	s'engageait dans un parking, un lieu privé, un chemin de terre — *entering a car park, private grounds, a track*	5 ☐
☐ 6	s'engageait sur une place à sens giratoire	6 ☐
☐ 7	roulait sur une place à sens giratoire	7 ☐
☐ 8	heurtait à l'arrière, en roulant dans le même sens et sur une même file	8 ☐

VÉHICULE B *VEHICLE B*

6 Preneur d'assurance / assuré / *Detail of insured (see insurance certificate)*
NOM : / *Name*
Prénom : / *First name*
Adresse / *Address*
Code postal : / *Postal code* — Pays. / *Country*
Tél. ou email / *Tel. or email*

7 Véhicule *vehicle*

A MOTEUR *VEHICLE*	REMORQUE *TRAILER*
Marque, type *Make, type*	
N° d'immatriculation *Registration number*	N° d'immatriculation *Registration number*
Pays d'immatriculation *Country of registration*	Pays d'immatriculation *Country of registration*

8 Société d'assurance (voir attestation d'assurance / see insurance certificate) / *Insurance company*
NOM : / *Name*
N° de contrat : / *Policy N°*

The *constat à l'amiable* form

If you want to be better prepared than us, you can download and print off a European Accident Statement (or EAS) form or ask your insurer to send you one. This, like the *constat à l'amiable* form, is a standard way of the parties recording what took place in the accident and is widely used across Europe. Be careful to only sign the form if you agree with what the other people have written on it (not easy if it's in French). The EAS form has advice on what to do in the event of an accident. In summary, it advises this:

- Stay calm, be polite and don't admit liability.
- Call 100 to contact the police and ambulance, if the severity of any injuries justifies it. You have to then wait for the police to arrive, even if it wasn't your fault.
- Photograph the scene. Make sure you include the number plates of all vehicles involved.
- If you're blocking traffic, move the vehicles once you've taken photos. If necessary, mark the corners of the vehicles with chalk or tape before moving them.
- Make some notes and a drawing of what happened.
- Get names and addresses of witnesses if you can.
- Exchange your insurance details with the other parties involved.
- Contact your insurer and send them the EAS or similar form if you complete one.

Obviously if you're unable to continue your journey, you'll need to contact your insurer and breakdown recovery. You might be without your vehicle for some time while it's repaired. If it's safe to do so, we'd suggest using any time spent waiting for recovery to find a hotel, pack clothes, toiletries, documents, valuables etc. Also have a think about what to do with food in your fridge and freezer, and this might have to be turned off in a repair shop.

UK Duty Free Allowances

While the UK doesn't have restrictions on importing meat or dairy from France, it does have duty free allowances. Each passenger over the age of 18 can import the following for personal use or as a gift, without declaring them or paying duty:

<table>
<tr><th>Goods</th><th>Allowance Per Passenger</th></tr>
<tr><td>Alcohol</td><td>How much you can bring depends on the type of alcohol.
You can bring in:<ul><li>beer - 42 litres</li><li>wine (still) - 18 litres</li></ul>You can also bring in either:<ul><li>spirits and other liquors over 22% alcohol - 4 litres</li><li>sparkling wine, fortified wine (for example port, sherry) and other alcoholic drinks up to 22% alcohol (not including beer or still wine) - 9 litres</li></ul>You can split this last allowance, for example you could bring 4.5 litres of fortified wine and 2 litres of spirits (both half of your allowance).</td></tr>
<tr><td>Tobacco</td><td>You can bring in one from the following:<ul><li>200 cigarettes</li><li>100 cigarillos</li><li>50 cigars</li><li>250g tobacco</li><li>200 sticks of tobacco for electronic heated tobacco devices</li></ul>You can split this allowance - so you could bring in 100 cigarettes and 25 cigars (both half of your allowance).</td></tr>
<tr><td>Other Goods</td><td>You can bring in other goods worth up to £390 (or up to £270 if you arrive by private plane or boat).</td></tr>
</table>

See this website for more details:

www.gov.uk/bringing-goods-into-uk-personal-use/arriving-in-Great-Britain

Getting the Ferry or Tunnel Home

Our satnav has car ferry ports and the Channel Tunnel entrance as points of interest, which is useful when planning a route to the port. If you're using the Tunnel, the GPS co-ordinates for the Calais terminal are: N50.936315, E1.814964.

Your company will tell you when they expect you to be at the port or tunnel, usually 30 minutes to an hour before you're due to leave. The process is roughly the same as the one you took when leaving the UK.

If you have a pet, the authorities at ferry check-in will usually hand you a device to scan your pet's microchip, to ensure it matches that in the passport. At the tunnel you'll need to take your pet to the Pet Reception building, no less than an hour before your train is due to depart. If you're leaving at night this building may be closed, look for the Night Time Pet Check-In instead.

Driving off the ferry at Dover, you're back in the UK!

Escorted Tours Abroad

If, after reading all of this, you'd like more support or company on your first trip abroad, you could consider a guided or escorted tour. The Caravan and Motorhome Club, for example, offers 'First Time' tours which start at campsites in the UK before taking you to campsites abroad and finally back to the UK. They include ferries, a course on driving on the right and a pack of essentials like high vis jackets, headlight adaptors and the like. See *www.caravanclub.co.uk* for more information and costs.

Thank you for buying and reading our book, we really appreciate it and hope it inspires you to head off and enjoy France in your motorhome.

If you have enjoyed the book or found it useful, **please take a moment to leave us a review on Amazon**. These really help other readers and give us feedback too on how we can improve later editions.

About the Authors

Julie and Jason Buckley quit work just before they turned 40 in 2011, to take a once in a lifetime, one-year tour of Europe in their motorhome. Documenting their travels on their blog *ourtour.co.uk*, two years later they finally returned home. Yearning for more adventures, they set a goal to change their lives and become financially free, enabling them to travel whenever they wanted to.

Aged 43, they 'retired' and took to the road once more to explore from the North Cape in Norway to the Sahara Desert in Morocco. They now mix up their time between motorhome life and their base in Nottinghamshire, England. Julie and Jason have written several books to help and inspire others to follow their own motorhome dreams or to start their own journey to financial freedom.

Other Books by the Authors

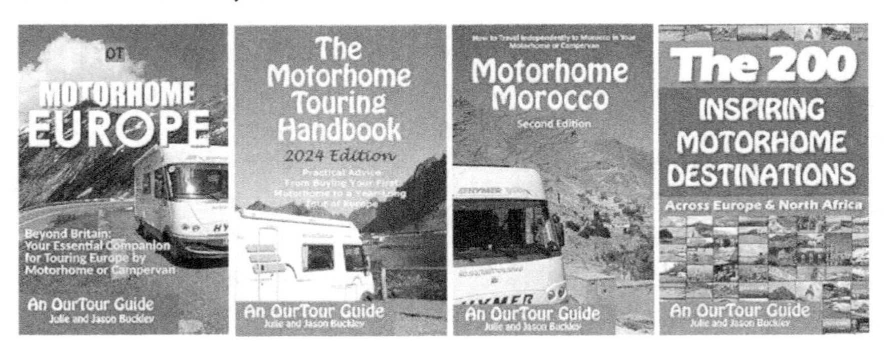

Julie and Jason have published several books, available from Amazon:

- **Motorhome Europe** – A full-colour guide offering both practical advice and inspiration for travel outside Britain to over 30 countries across Europe from Ireland to Greece, Portugal to Norway.
- **The Motorhome Touring Handbook** – Packed full of practical advice from choosing a motorhome and touring the UK to travelling abroad or planning for and enjoying a year-long tour.
- **Motorhome Morocco** – The book we wanted to buy before our first trip to Morocco! It guides you through the process of planning and enjoying a tour of this incredible North African country.
- **The 200** – 200 of the most memorable, inspirational and interesting places we've stayed, in over a decade of motorhome touring.
- **A Monkey Ate My Breakfast** – A travelogue of our first motorhome tour of Morocco in 2011, an eye-opening adventure onto a new continent, and into a new and exotic culture.
- **The Non-Trepreneurs** – A practical guide explaining how we think about and manage our personal finances to enable us to retire aged 43, and travel whenever we want.
- **OurTour Downloaded** – All the blog posts from our first year of full-time motorhome touring, handily gathered into one ebook.

When not travelling, Julie and Jason live in a small town outside Nottingham in the UK. To get in touch, or follow future travels, any of these will work:

- **Email**: julieandjason@ourtour.co.uk
- **Web**: ourtour.co.uk
- **Youtube**: search *youtube.com* for 'ourtour blog'
- **Instagram**: www.instagram.com/ourtourblog
- **Twitter**: @ourtourblog
- **Facebook**: search *facebook.com* for 'ourtour blog'

Things Change and We Make Mistakes...

We've tried our best to make this a useful and accurate book. We're human though and will make mistakes. Also, some of the book is very much our personal opinion, which others are 100% certain to disagree with! Things change, and some sections will date quickly, even with new editions being published.

If there's anything in here which could have a big impact on your safety, financial situation or happiness, please do your own independent research before taking action. The websites we've referenced throughout (*in italics*) have a wealth of information available, some of which will be more up-to-date than this book.

If you spot any glaring errors or obvious missed topics, please drop us a line at *julieandjason@ourtour.co.uk* and we'll be forever grateful and will of course correct future editions.

Reference Information

The following sections provide information which you might want to reference before or during your trip to France.

Useful French Words

You don't need to memorise these words, but it's worth scanning through them before you go, just so you're familiar with them.

French	English
Aire de Service	Service Point and/or Overnight Parking
Allumez vos Feux	Turn Your Headlights On
Autoroute	Motorway
Bouchon	Traffic Jam
Brouillard	Fog
Cales	Levelling Ramps
Camping-Car	Motorhome
Carte Bleu or CB	Generic term for credit and debit cards
Carte Grise	V5C Log Book
Chimiques	Chemicals
Col	Mountain Pass
Distributeur de Billets	Cash Machine (ATM)
Douane	Customs
Eau Grise	Grey (Used) Water
Eau Noire	Black (WC/Cassette) Water
Eau Potable	Drinking Water
En Pente	Sloping
Fermé	Closed
Freins	Brakes
Gratuit	Free
Hors Gel	Frost Protection (the water is turned off)
Interdit	Forbidden
Médecin	Doctor
Moteur	Engine
Neige	Snow
Ouvert	Open
Pare-Brise	Windscreen

French	English
Péage	Toll
Petite Monnaie	Small Change
Pharmacie	Chemist
Pneu	Tyre
Rappel	Reminder, 'remember the speed limit'
Remorque	Trailer
Vent	Wind

Packing Checklist

The following list is personalised to our needs but should be a good starting point for any trip. We use this checklist to ensure we haven't forgotten anything vital, like our potato masher or corkscrew!

Legal Bits

There are things that you are legally required to carry in some countries that we don't have to carry in the UK. It's best to check the AA or RAC website for an up-to-date list of what you need for France, and any other countries you're going to. Legally, you need to carry these items on your motorhome:

- ☐ UK Sticker or numberplates with UK identifier
- ☐ Angles Morts Stickers (over 3,500kg only)
- ☐ Emergency Warning Triangle
- ☐ High Visibility Jacket (one per passenger, must be accessible from the inside the van)
- ☐ Headlight Adjusters

The following items aren't mandatory, but we recommend them:

- ☐ Spare Bulb Kit
- ☐ First Aid Kit
- ☐ Fire Extinguisher
- ☐ Spare Glasses or Contact Lenses
- ☐ Bike Rack Signal Board - red and white striped (only if you have a bike rack and plan to carry on into Spain or Italy)
- ☐ Smoke/CO Alarm (again not a legal requirement, but get one anyway for your own safety)

Documentation

We know it's boring, but there are some documents you'll need to take with you and others it will be handy to have in case of a problem. These items are legally required:

- ☐ Passports
- ☐ Card Driving Licenses
- ☐ V5C (your motorhome's 'log book' - must be the original, not an electronic scan or photocopy)
- ☐ Motorhome Insurance Certificate (ensure they cover all the countries you'll pass through for entire duration of your trip)
- ☐ Animal Health Certificate (if your four-legged friend is going abroad with you) or Northern Ireland Pet Passport
- ☐ An ETIAS visa waiver for each traveller (needed from some point in 2025, it's not yet clear when)
- ☐ You don't need to carry an insurance green card or international driver's permits (IDPs) for France

These items aren't legally needed in France, but we suggest you carry them anyway:

- ☐ GHICs - Global Health Insurance Cards (these are free, and enable you to access local health cover in the EU)
- ☐ Photocopies of all documentation (kept somewhere safe; we also scanned ours and emailed them to ourselves – you could also simply photograph them)
- ☐ Motorhome Instructions (always handy for troubleshooting as stuff inevitably packs up while you're away)
- ☐ Breakdown Cover
- ☐ Mobile Phone contract details (if in contract, these are handy for bill queries and renewing)
- ☐ ACSI Discount CampingCard or app (gives you discounted stay at campsites out of season across Europe)
- ☐ PASS'ETAPES card if you plan to use Camping-Car Parks (you can buy this at your first site if you like)
- ☐ Your *télépéage* transponder if you don't want to pay for toll roads with cash/card
- ☐ Spending Book (if you're on a budget a small book to track all your spending is a big help)

Daily Servicing

Once you're on the road you'll need a few items to keep you in supplies you'd normally take for granted in a house, such as water, electricity and gas.

- ☐ Hose Pipe (you can get collapsible ones, but we prefer a length of 'normal' hose pipe)
- ☐ Tap Connectors (we use Hozelock-style ones. 1/2", 3/4" and 1" screw threads, plus a male-to-male connector cover most taps)
- ☐ Collapsible Water Carrier or Watering Can (sometimes you can't connect or get near enough to the tap to use your hose, or don't want to move your van)
- ☐ Funnel (you'll probably need one to get the water into your tank if you use a water carrier rather than a watering can. We once fashioned a flat, fold-around one from the lid of an ice-cream tub)
- ☐ Power Hook-Up Cable (we don't often use mains power, so only have a single 15 metre, 2.5mm, 16A cable. If you rely on mains more than us, consider carrying a longer cable, or two cables. Remember to unwind them fully when in heavy use to avoid over heating)
- ☐ Hook Up Cable 2 Pin Adapter (some French campsites and aires still use the two-pin plug as opposed to the blue European three-pin)
- ☐ A reverse polarity detector and correction adapter cable (to ensure your mains appliances stay safe)
- ☐ Electric Fan Heater (we use ours on hook-up to heat the van. In sub-zero conditions we also use the gas heating to stop water freezing in the van)
- ☐ 'Dish' Style LPG Connection Adapter if you have refillable LPG
- ☐ Grey/Waste Water Tank Fresh (trust us, when it gets hot the grey tank can smell! We've used the official stuff, but now tend to use dissolved dishwasher tablets or a bottle of cheap cola)
- ☐ Fresh Water Tank Cleaner and Purifier (to keep your fresh water tank clean, either that or drink bottled water while travelling - we use 5 litre water bottles and refill them at service points)
- ☐ Spirit Level (for ensuring your van is level and to work out where to place the levelling ramps)
- ☐ Levelling Ramps (as car parks and aires nearly always slope when you want to sleep in them!)
- ☐ Wheel Chocks (we've used these in a couple of very steep places to give us some comfort we wouldn't roll off the mountain!)

- ☐ Anti-Slip Mats (handy if you get stuck on grass or sand)

Navigation and Finding Places to Sleep

Below are the tools we use for navigation and finding places to sleep.

- ☐ Satnav (love or hate it, without a satnav driving isn't as easy. We have an OHREX truck satnav) check it has maps for France
- ☐ Paper Road Atlas (don't fully trust your satnav as they love short cuts, great for cars but not motorhomes. We always have a paper map for the country too and use it to check out the route suggested by satnav before we set off). We use the spiral-bound Michelin Touring & Motorist Atlas for France
- ☐ Highlighter Pen (track your progress on the paper map and create a great reminder of your trip, for the more tech-savvy, you can record and share your route with apps like Polarsteps or Travelboast)
- ☐ Phrase Books (so you can ask for directions anywhere, although translation apps are much better if you have a smartphone)
- ☐ Organic Maps (free smartphone app useful for navigation if you have satnav issues, or when away from the van - download the maps for all the areas of France you plan to visit while on WiFi to save your data allowance)
- ☐ Apps for overnight stays (we mainly use *park4night* and *campercontact* and we've paid for the offline versions so we can use them without internet access).
- ☐ Books for overnight stays, like Camperstop or All the Aires
- ☐ Compass (handy for working out which way the sun will come up and manually orienting satellite dishes). Our watch has one built-in.

Outdoors, another Room to Your Motorhome

Motorhomes aren't huge, but once parked up on a campsite the outdoors becomes an extra room, you just need to furnish it accordingly.

- ☐ Camping Chairs
- ☐ Camping Table
- ☐ Foldaway BBQ, Gas BBQ or Gas Stove (we've used all three, but currently use a gas stove as we can take it anywhere)
- ☐ BBQ Tools
- ☐ Picnic Rug
- ☐ Sunglasses / Prescription Sunglasses

- ☐ Insect Repellent
- ☐ Mosquito net (we carry this but haven't yet needed it in France)
- ☐ Citronella Candles (help keep the mozzies away, again not usually an issue in France)
- ☐ Fly Swat (for the middle of the night cull)
- ☐ Umbrellas (we won't lie to you, it's not always sunny. We have a large golf umbrella and two fold-up small ones)

Tools and Things for Fixing Stuff

We've needed to do quite a few repairs on our longer tours. Even if your van is new, it's good to have a few tools and bits to fix to stuff with.

- ☐ Ratchet Socket Set
- ☐ Multi Tool
- ☐ WD-40 Lubricant
- ☐ Assorted Cable Ties
- ☐ Gaffa Tape (also called Duct Tape)
- ☐ Super Glue (either lots of little tubes or a decent reseal-able bottle)
- ☐ Spare Fuses
- ☐ Multi-Meter (useful when making repairs on the 12V system)
- ☐ Wheel Brace
- ☐ Vehicle Jack
- ☐ Precision Screwdriver Set
- ☐ Standard Screwdriver Set
- ☐ Spanner Set
- ☐ Torch (LED ones last ages - we're often amazed at how dark it gets in some places we park!)
- ☐ Tow Rope (we no longer carry one, but it's something to consider)
- ☐ Spare Engine Oil
- ☐ Disposable Gloves
- ☐ Anti-Gel Winter Fuel Additive (consider taking some if you're going into the mountains in winter)
- ☐ All-Season Screen Wash (for topping up your van's washer bottle)

Kitchen Essentials

We stock our van with a lot of items from the kitchen of our house. But there are a few items we've bought especially for the trip.

- ☐ Melamine Plates and Bowls (they weigh less and don't break)
- ☐ Mugs (any sort, but the more stable the better)
- ☐ Wine Glasses (we used to use plastic ones, big mistake, even cheap wine tastes so much better from a glass)
- ☐ Plastic/Acrylic Glasses (for drinks other than wine, less glass means less noise and breakages on bumpy roads)
- ☐ Water/Wine Jug (a small jug to decant wine from a box, for when we want to feel posh or have guests!)
- ☐ Plastic Food Storage Boxes (collect as many as you can - our pasta, rice, cereal etc is in upright ones, flat ones are used to house potentially leaky stuff and to stop stuff moving around)
- ☐ Double Skillet & Diffuser (we no longer carry this, but it's something to consider, have a look at *www.thedoubleskilletpancompany.com*) or search Amazon for the Ridgemonkey, a similar product)
- ☐ Large Frying Pan (if you're not taking a double skillet. Measure the width of cupboard it's going in, and the dimension of the pan across the top, not the base to ensure it will fit)
- ☐ Small Frying Pan
- ☐ Pan Protector Matting
- ☐ Large Saucepan
- ☐ Stackable Saucepan and Steamer Pans (so we can cook potatoes and steam veg on a single hob ring)
- ☐ Remoska (a 230V oven, see *www.remoska.co.uk*)
- ☐ Oven Proof Dishes (we don't have an oven, but if you do you'll need some!)
- ☐ Oven Gloves (even with no oven, we still use them for hot stuff)
- ☐ Gas Hob Kettle (for when we aren't hooked up to electricity)
- ☐ Low Wattage Kettle (for when we are hooked up to electricity)
- ☐ A Hot Water Flask (if we're on hook-up, we boil water before leaving the site to make hot drinks during the day, saving our gas)
- ☐ Cafetière or on hob Espresso Maker
- ☐ Chopping Board
- ☐ Cheese Grater
- ☐ Measuring Jug (decent size, plastic or acrylic)
- ☐ Compact Weighing Scales
- ☐ Cutlery (make sure you have plenty of teaspoons - they vanish)

- ☐ Scissors (at least a couple of pairs)
- ☐ Tin Opener
- ☐ Vegetable Peeler (also handy for shaving Parmesan cheese!)
- ☐ Bottle Opener/Cork Screw (this should be at the top of the list...)
- ☐ Bread Knife (as un-sliced loaves are cheaper and last longer)
- ☐ Sharp Cutting Knife
- ☐ Wooden Spoons
- ☐ Spatula
- ☐ Serving Spoon
- ☐ Wooden Skewers (good for marshmallow toasting, making kebabs and poking at/fixing stuff stuff)
- ☐ Potato Masher
- ☐ Cigarette Lighter/Matches (for lighting the hob if the ignition fails, or a BBQ)
- ☐ Cleaning Sponges
- ☐ Cleaning Wipes (we use antibacterial wipes for cleaning the van as well as the taps and hoses at water points)
- ☐ Cleaning Scourers
- ☐ Normal Household Cleaning Products
- ☐ Washing Up Liquid
- ☐ Universal Sink Plug (as every campsite sink has a different sized plug hole)
- ☐ Dustpan and Brush
- ☐ Mini 12V Vacuum Cleaner
- ☐ Antibacterial Hand Wash (for your hands after emptying the loo!)
- ☐ Kitchen Roll
- ☐ Tin Foil
- ☐ Cling Film
- ☐ Freezer Bags
- ☐ Ice Cube Bags or Tray (for those long hot summer days!)
- ☐ Bottle Holders (free supermarket cardboard ones reduce clinking)

Store Cupboard Food Items

While we're in the kitchen it's worth having a few items always in your van, so you can have a cuppa at any time! We won't list loads of things, as each person has different tastes, but a few tins (soup, beans?) along with some teabags, coffee, stock cubes, gravy granules (we can't find these anywhere abroad), UHT milk, a bottle of water, a bottle or two of wine, salt and pepper, vinegar, ketchup and chocolate would never go to waste in our van!

Bathroom

- ☐ Micro-towelling Towels (they feel like normal towels but dry really fast so less damp towels hanging up around the van)
- ☐ Toothbrush
- ☐ Toothpaste
- ☐ Toiletries
- ☐ Soap
- ☐ Toilet Rolls (you can get special motorhome ones, but we use the cheaper two-ply ones and they work fine)
- ☐ Chemical Toilet Fluids (unless you have a SOG unit - see *www.soguk.co.uk*)
- ☐ Air Freshener
- ☐ Medications
- ☐ Contact Lenses
- ☐ Shaving Kit
- ☐ Ear Plugs (even the best campsite can be noisy)
- ☐ Sunscreen and Aftersun
- ☐ Nailbrush
- ☐ Bags For Life (campsite showers rarely have enough hooks for all your clothes. Large supermarket bags for life - one of the thicker plastic ones with fabric handles - hang on a hook keeping all our clothes and towels dry)

Bedroom & Soft Furnishings

- ☐ Pillows
- ☐ Duvet (we have a summer tog duvet with an unzipped sleeping bag on top of it, then a blanket on top of that, so we can use whatever combination we need to keep warm/cool)
- ☐ Memory Foam Mattress Topper (even beds made up from the chair cushions are comfortable with one of these, so you can imagine how lovely our pull-down bed is with one on it - sleep heaven)
- ☐ Bed Sheets (a normal and brushed cotton one for cold weather)
- ☐ Spare Set of Bedding (you can't always wash and dry in a day)
- ☐ Blankets (great for curling up under when the weather isn't warm)
- ☐ Cushions (add a bit of comfort and colour to your van on one go)

- ☐ Sofa Throws (we use these on the seat parts of the sofas as they're easy to wash and clean)
- ☐ Hot Water Bottle

Clothing and Laundry

This was a tricky one for our longer tours as we would be travelling through most types of weather. We have one shelf each in the wardrobe, one hook each and a cupboard each - in it we have to squeeze everything from ski jackets and thermals to swim wear and wetsuit.

We've found 'technical' clothing to be really good as its quick-drying and doesn't need ironing. Check out the camping and hiking sections in shops or online and you'll be amazed at what is out there - we even found a shirt impregnated with mosquito repellent! Here's an example lady's packing list:

- ☐ Jeans x 2
- ☐ Quick Drying Trousers
- ☐ Zip Off Trouser/Shorts
- ☐ Shorts x 3
- ☐ Skirts x 2
- ☐ T Shirts x 8
- ☐ Vest Tops x 8
- ☐ Polo Shirt
- ☐ Fleece x 2
- ☐ Mosquito Repellent Shirt
- ☐ Quick Drying Shirts x 2
- ☐ Long Sleeved Tops x 4
- ☐ Going Out Tops x 2
- ☐ Fleece/Hooded Jacket
- ☐ Swimwear (Bikini, Sarong, Beach Shoes, Wetsuit!)
- ☐ Sun Hat or Baseball Cap
- ☐ Winter wear (Thermal Leggings, Thermal Top, Ski Jacket)
- ☐ Scarf
- ☐ Gloves
- ☐ Woolly Hat
- ☐ Knickers
- ☐ Bras (1 x black, 1 x flesh, 1 x other)
- ☐ Socks (Thick Ski Socks, Trainer Socks, Walking Socks and Socks!)
- ☐ Pyjamas / Nightie

- ☐ Walking Boots
- ☐ Trainers
- ☐ Flip Flops
- ☐ Going Out Shoes
- ☐ Gilet
- ☐ Waterproof / Going Out Jacket

Don't forget all those bits and pieces you need to keep your clothes clean if you're going away for a while.

- ☐ Laundry Sack/Bag
- ☐ Washing Liquid/Powder
- ☐ Fabric Softener
- ☐ Coins for the Machines (save €1 coins)
- ☐ Clothes Line
- ☐ Pegs (you can never have too many of them, you'll be amazed!)
- ☐ Drying Rack (whatever kind you can fit into your van, we use a Folding Sock Dryer which we affectionately call our 'pant chandelier' it either hangs off the bike rack or in the bathroom if the weather is bad)

Entertainment, Leisure and Tech

- ☐ Books
- ☐ Kindle/eReader (we have a Kindle as we could never carry that many physical books in our motorhome - it's great!)
- ☐ Board Games (we play Scrabble if you do too bring a dictionary to settle any arguments!)
- ☐ Playing Cards
- ☐ Chess Set (unused!)
- ☐ Snorkelling Kit
- ☐ Fishing Gear and Crab Line
- ☐ Travel Journal (notes of your adventures make a brilliant keepsake)
- ☐ Pens and Pencil
- ☐ Paper Pads (for scribbling notes or lists)
- ☐ Music (CDs or MP3s as the local radio stations are generally pants, unless you like the 80s)
- ☐ TV (ours plays from a USB memory stick, and has a built-in DVD player and FreeSat decoder, plus we use an Amazon Fire TV Stick to watch streaming internet TV)
- ☐ Laptop (preferably with a long battery life)

- ☐ External Hard Drive (to store all your photos)
- ☐ MiFi Personal 4G to WiFi Hotspot
- ☐ Multi-Country Internet and Phone SIMs
- ☐ Mobile Phones
- ☐ Films/TV Series (either DVDs or electronically saved they're ideal for long nights or rainy days)
- ☐ Headphones (to watch TV without disturbing others in the van)
- ☐ USB Memory Sticks/SD Cards (for storing / sharing photos and files)
- ☐ Chargers for Everything (12V if possible, for lower current draw)
- ☐ Power Plug Adapters (our van has a couple of two-pin plugs so we have one of these permanently plugged in and a spare for when we're out and about)
- ☐ Alarm Clock (we thought we wouldn't need one, but we ended up sleeping later and later each day)
- ☐ Binoculars
- ☐ Spare Batteries
- ☐ Bicycle (as you can't always park close to what you want to see)
- ☐ Cycle Helmet (obligatory in some countries)
- ☐ Bicycle Pump
- ☐ Puncture Repair Kit
- ☐ Christmas Lights and Decorations (if you're away over Christmas)
- ☐ Bunting/National Flag (for special occasions!)

Pampered Pooch

Our Cavalier King Charles Spaniel, Charlie, was our surrogate child so he got very pampered. He had his own space in the van, and his own cupboard for his toys, treats and medication.

- ☐ Bed
- ☐ Blankets
- ☐ Non-Spill Water Bowl
- ☐ Food Bowl
- ☐ Travel (Collapsible) Water Bowl
- ☐ Dry Food (we bought the cheapest from the supermarkets, less additives and he loved it, and swapping between foods seemed to have no effect on him)
- ☐ Tinned Food (again the cheapest, he loved all of them)
- ☐ Tick & Flea Treatment (check with your vet so you get the best medication for where you are travelling to - Charlie either had spot on Advantix or a Scalibor collar as both repels ticks, fleas,

mosquitoes and importantly protect against leishmaniasis, which is endemic in continental Europe)

- ☐ Tick Removers (even though his treatment repelled them, he still got the odd tick so we needed these to remove them)
- ☐ Worming Tablets
- ☐ Claw Clippers
- ☐ Fur Clippers
- ☐ Comb/Brush
- ☐ Ear Cleaner
- ☐ Shampoo
- ☐ Dog Towel (microfibre for quick drying - trust us you don't want you pooch borrowing your towel after a day on the beach!)
- ☐ Lead and Spare Lead
- ☐ Collar
- ☐ Harness (an alternative to a collar but can also be used to restrain your pooch while you drive)
- ☐ Identity Disc (ensure it has the UK dialling code before your phone number if you're going abroad)
- ☐ Coat (pampered pooch never liked being cold)
- ☐ Toys
- ☐ Treats
- ☐ Poo Bags (never underestimate how many of these you'll get through on a trip! Some towns in France do provide them for free in parks and cities so keep your eyes peeled)

Enhancements to Your Van

You can add numerous things to your motorhome to make life more comfortable on the road.

- ☐ Non-Slip Matting (for every cupboard)
- ☐ Blackout Thermal Curtain Linings
- ☐ 12V DC to 230V AC Power Inverter (for charging all your gadgets that don't have a 12V charger, running clippers and the like. We have a 300W pure-sine inverter which works well for us.)
- ☐ Windscreen Thermal Cover/Silver Screens (internal or external screens help keep your van warm or cool, we use external ones)
- ☐ Solar Panel and Charge Controller
- ☐ Additional Leisure Battery (an alternative or addition to adding solar panels is adding another leisure battery)

- ☐ Habitation Door Fly Screen (our current van has a built-in screen, but you can buy after-market ones too)
- ☐ LPG Tank(s) (refillable tanks or bottles which take LPG/GPL/Autogas are a big help on a multi-country trip as there is no gas bottle standardisation across Europe)
- ☐ SOG Unit
- ☐ Satellite Dish (if you want to watch live UK TV on the road, although you can often do this with the internet these days)

Useful Sources of Information

This appendix lists some of the useful sources of information we've used to plan our motorhome tours across France.

Motorhome Forums

- **Motorhome Facts** - *motorhomefacts.com* - a very well-established forum. Searchable for free. Annual fee if you want to ask or answer questions.
- **Motorhome Fun** - *motorhomefun.co.uk* - again a very useful forum. Searchable for free. Annual fee if you want to ask or answer questions.
- **Out and About Live** - *www.outandaboutlive.co.uk* - run by Warners Group Publications who publish Motorhome Monthly Magazine.
- **Facebook Groups** - there are loads of free groups on Facebook, for specific makes of motorhome for example - we're in the Hymer Owners Group. All offer useful information, some have negotiated discounts with insurers.

Motorhome Magazines

- **Motorhome Monthly Magazine (MMM)** - an iconic magazine in the UK motorhome world, covering a broad range of topics including tour stories.
- **Practical Motorhome** - another widely-available motorhome magazine in the UK. Focuses on the practical aspects of motorhome life.

Overnight French Motorhome Stopovers

- **All the Aires** - maps and details of official aires across Europe created and published by Vicarious Media (*www.vicarious-shop.com*). Focussed on France, Spain, Portugal, Belgium, Luxembourg and the Netherlands.
- **France Passion** - *www.france-passion.com* - again available through Vicarious Media. The book is refreshed each year. Buying that year's book gives you access to free camping at French vineyards, farms, restaurants etc. In practice you can usually use a book for the following year or two too.
- **Camperstop Europe** - *www.camperstop.com* - book and smartphone app listing thousands of aires across Europe.
- **Camper Contact** - *www.campercontact.com* - website and app again listing aires across Europe.
- **Park4Night** - *park4night.com* - website and app listing both official and unofficial (free and wild camping) overnight stops across Europe.
- **ACSI Camping Card** - *www.campingcard.co.uk* - the card is included with books giving off-season discounts at over 3,000 campsites across Europe.
- **The Guide Officiel Camping et Caravaning France** - available on *amazon.co.uk* - a guide to over 8,000 French campsites (French language only).

Legal Driving Requirements Abroad

- **The AA** - *www.theaa.com* - search the site for 'Driving in France for tons of advice on what you legally need to carry, rules of the road, use of lights during the day and so on.
- **The RAC** - *www.rac.co.uk* - again has a very useful section covering what you legally need to know and carry when driving in France, and advice on staying safe on the road.
- **The Caravan and Motorhome Club** - *www.caravanclub.co.uk* - look in the Overseas Holidays section.
- **The Camping and Caravanning Club** - *campingandcaravanningclub.co.uk* - search for 'European Travel Advice'.

Getting at Your Money Abroad

- **Halifax** - *www.halifax.co.uk* - we use their Clarity credit card abroad for making fuel and other card purchases.
- **Nationwide Bank** - *www.nationwide.co.uk* - we use the debit account card for this account, which comes with European breakdown cover and travel insurance, for making fee-free cash withdrawals abroad.
- **Caxton FX** - *www.caxtonfx.com* - we used to use the Caxton Prepaid Currency Card for making non-cash purchases abroad but now have a Nationwide current account.

Internet Access in the UK and Abroad

- **Motorhome WiFi** - *www.motorhomewifi.com* - these guys sell specialised motorhome equipment and SIM cards for internet access in your van.
- **Popit Mobile** - *www.popitmobile.co.uk*– as of autumn 2023 the only UK provider we know to officially offer 100GB a month, all of which can be used in France and the rest of the EU.
- **Prepaid SIM Data Card Wiki** - *prepaid-data-sim-card.wikia.com* - a useful resource if you choose to buy a French SIM card rather than using a UK-based SIM.
- **VPN for Watching iPlayer** - *techradar.com/vpn/bbc-iplayer-vpn* - if you want to access BBC iPlayer and other UK-only websites from abroad you may need a VPN, especially if using campsite WiFi or a French SIM.

Motorhome Insurance

- **Safeguard** - *www.safeguarduk.co.uk*
- **Adrian Flux** - *www.adrianflux.co.uk*
- **Comfort** - *www.comfort-insurance.co.uk*
- **Caravan Guard** - *www.caravanguard.co.uk*
- **Saga (drivers over 50s only)** - *www.saga.co.uk*
- **Camping and Caravanning Club** (members only) - *www.campingandcaravanningclub.co.uk*
- **Caravan and Motorhome Club Insurance** (members only) - *www.caravanclub.co.uk*

Calor Gas and Self-Refillable LPG Systems

- **Calor Gas** - *www.calor.co.uk*
- **Safefill Self-Refillable LPG Bottles** - *www.safefill.co.uk*
- **Gaslow Self-Refillable LPG Bottles** - *gaslowdirect.com*
- **Alugas Self-Refillable LPG Bottles** - *www.autogasleisure.co.uk*
- **Finding LPG stations:** *www.mylpg.eu* and *www.lpgstations.com*

Low Emission Zones and Other Urban Access Zones

- **General advice on which zones exist** - *urbanaccessregulations.eu* and *www.green-zones.eu*
- **Obtaining a French Crit'Air vignette** - *www.certificat-air.gouv.fr*

Printed in Great Britain
by Amazon